# Apple Pro Training Series:
## Shake 4 Quick-Reference Guide

Damian Allen

Apple Pro Training Series: Shake 4 Quick-Reference Guide

Published by Peachpit Press. For information on Peachpit Press books, contact:

Peachpit Press
1249 Eighth Street
Berkeley, CA 94710
(510) 524-2178
Fax: (510) 524-2221
http://www.peachpit.com

To report errors, please send a note to errata@peachpit.com
Peachpit Press is a division of Pearson Education

Contributing Writers: Damian Allen, Peter Warner, Angus Taggart

ISBN 0-321-38246-3

9 8 7 6 5 4 3 2 1

Printed and bound in the United States of America

# Table of Contents

Interface

Image

Color

Filter

Key

Layer

Transform

Warp

Other

Scripting

Customizing

Keyboard

## Shake Navigation

The development team for Shake went to great pains to make sure there were as few keyboard shortcuts to learn as possible. So the same keyboard and mouse navigation controls can be used pretty much everywhere in the Shake interface—the Node Workspace, the Viewer Workspace, the Curve Editor, et cetera. These shortcuts are *location sensitive*, so pressing the same key or mouse combination will affect the interface differently depending on where your mouse pointer was when you initiated the shortcut.

Here are the main navigation shortcuts you need to know:

**LMB**
(Left Mouse Button)

**MMB**
(Middle Mouse Button)
On a scroll wheel mouse
(shown), depress the scroll
wheel itself.

**RMB**
(Right Mouse Button)

To pan a view:
**a)** Click and drag the **MMB** OR,
**b)** Hold down the **OPTION** key and click and drag the **LMB**

To scale a view in *discrete steps*:
Press the + or – keys on the main keyboard.

To scale a view in *freeform style*:
**a)** Hold down the **CTRL** and **OPTION** keys and click and drag the **LMB** left and right OR,
**b)** Hold down the **OPTION** and **COMMAND** keys and click and drag the **LMB** left and right, OR,
**c)** Hold down the **CTRL** *or* **COMMAND** key and click and drag the **MMB** left and right.

Press the **HOME** key to bring the view back to a 100% scale

Press the **F** key to frame the selected nodes in the Node Workspace. In the Viewer Workspace, press the **F** key to zoom out so that the currently loaded image fits entirely in the viewer space.

## The Shake Browser

Unlike most Apple software, Shake uses a UNIX-style text-only browser. Directories (or folders) are listed in order, starting with the root level of your computer's main hard drive. If you're looking for your Desktop, it's found inside the Users directory under your current login. So, if you're logged on as Jimmy, items on the desktop will be found in /Users/Jimmy/Desktop/. This is also where you'll find your personal documents—/Users/Jimmy/Documents/. A quick shortcut to your Users' directory, known as your **Home** folder, is to select **$HOME** from the directory drop-down menu in the Shake Browser.

If you're looking for footage or scripts anywhere other than your system hard drive—on a FireWire drive, a second hard drive, or a DVD-ROM for example—these devices will show up in a folder called /Volumes/ at the root level (the top of the list).

## Anatomy of a Browser Window

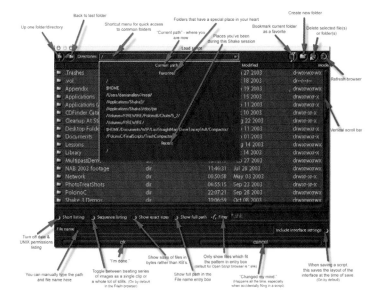

## Relative Paths

Shake's File Browser allows you to specify local (or *relative*) file paths. Relative file paths record the location of a file **relative to the main Shake script**. What this means is that as long as your Shake script and media maintain the same folder structure, you can easily move scripts and footage from one workstation to another, or even one facility to another, without encountering media relinking issues.

**Note:** in larger facilities, UNC file paths are usually preferred, since they allow access to footage in one server location from several client machines.

To use local paths, do the following:
1. Save your script
2. Choose the *Image - **FileIn*** node.
3. Activate the Relative Path control in the File Browser

4. Locate the file you wish to import
5. In the File Name field, add the relative path syntax (see below) that matches the location of the file relative to your saved script.

There are two important notations to use when entering a relative file path: `../` and `./`

**A)** `../` tells Shake to move up one directory (folder) from the directory in which the Shake script resides.

**Example 1**

To specify the file path of Shot08.mov in the Shake project MyScript.shk, you would enter the following into the File Name field of the FileIn Browser:

```
../Media/Shot08.mov
```

i.e. Shake is told to move up one directory from the Scripts directory, which sends it to the MyShakeProject directory. It then looks in the folder specified after the "../" which is Media, and finds the requested file Shot08.mov

**Example 2**

      Shot08.mov
      Shot12.mov
    Scripts
      DraftShots
        MyScript.shk

To specify the file path of Shot08.mov in the Shake project MyScript.shk, you would enter the following into the File Name field of the FileIn Browser:

```
../../Media/Shot08.mov
```

In this case Shake is told to move 2 directories up from the initial directory before tracking down the file.

**B)** . / Tells Shake to begin its search in the same directory as the Shake script.

**Example**

      Shot08.mov
      Shot12.mov

To specify the file path of Shot08.mov in the Shake project MyScript.shk, you would enter the following into the File Name field of the FileIn Browser:

```
./Media/Shot08.mov
```

**Tip:** to quickly change paths in a script to relative, use the find-and-replace features of a text editor (make sure it's set to plain text editing) to swap the extended file path for a file path using the above notation.

## Introduction to Premultiplication

Premultiplication becomes an issue when you color correct and then composite foreground footage. The term describes the relationship between the RGB channels and their associated mask.

### What is a premultiplied image?

A premultiplied element, which typically comes out of a 3D render, has its RGB channel multiplied by its Alpha. Therefore:
- If the Alpha is black, the RGB must be black.
- No RGB pixel can have a higher value than the corresponding Alpha pixel.

### Why does it exist?

The math of a composite (and the *KeyMix* node) is:

```
FgRGB * FgA + ((1-FgA) * BgRGB)
```

This indicates the foreground is multiplied by its alpha channel during the composite. When you color correct, you often modify your black levels, which forces you to re-multiply by your alpha. However, this has already been done on a premultiplied plate. Thus, you should first divide by the alpha (*Color – MDiv*), do your color correction, and then re-premultiply (*Color – MMult).*

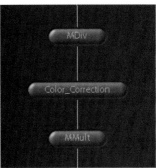

### How to deal with it
- Color correct unpremultiplied elements. Insert a *MDiv* before your color correction nodes. Then, place a *MMult* node after your color correction nodes.
- Transform or Filter premultiplied elements. Any other node that modifies RGBA evenly should ideally be done on a premultiplied element.

Typical problems when you ignore premultiplication include edges that get brighter on the antialiasing, or black areas of the image outside of the mask are boosted up. This image is incorrectly handled:

This image is correctly handled with an *MDiv*/Color correction/*MMult* string:

**The Infinite Workspace**

The infinite workspace is a Shake engine feature that allows you move images around and never worry if they will get clipped by moving outside of the frame borders.

Take any image, put a *Warp* *–Twirl* on it, and set your *startAngle* to 360. Then, apply a Transform – *Scale* node and scale it down by 50 percent. Because of the infinite workspace, the tendrils of the *Twirl* come into the frame in the following image.

When a Crop is inserted between the **Twirl** and the **ScaleScale**, the infinite workspace is broken:

**Exceptions**

Occasionally, you may get clipped elements as you move them around. If you do, check the following nodes:

| | |
|---:|:---|
| **Blur** | This has a toggle, *spread*, to control if you are working on the frame or outside of it. If you have blurred a mask, this node may clip the mask. Toggle *spread to outside frame*. |
| **Crop** | Clips the infinite workspace. If this is a problem, instead use a Viewport node, which has the same controls, but doesn't clip the frame. |
| **SetDOD** | Limits the area you have to work with, but doesn't change your resolution. |
| **SetBGColor** | Sets the color outside of the DOD (the green box). |

**Concatenation of Color Correctors and Transforms**

Concatenation collapses multiple operations into one function with internal calculations. This means you calculate with more accuracy and greater speed. For example, if you apply a **Brightness** operator, which multiplies color, and multiply everything by 5, and then apply a second **Brightness** operator and multiply by .2, it returns your original image. In non-concatenating operations, you have clamping, as no value would be higher than .2.

Shake concatenates certain adjacent operators from the Color or Transform tab. These nodes are marked by a C in the upper-left corner of the function button.

Masking breaks the concatenation. If you use the same mask several times, your problems are compounded:

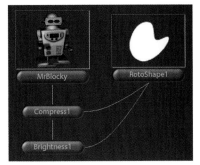

To fix the problem, rewire your tree to use a *Layer*-**KeyMix** instead:

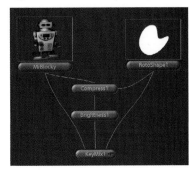

A good example of using concatenation is a simple color grading on Cineon plates. Here, **LogLin**, **ColorGrade** (a macro from "Cookbook - Color Macros") and **LogLin** all concatenate together, and preserve the highlights from the Cineon plate:

## Common Film and Broadcast Formats

The following table contains common film and broadcast formats. Note that all of the formats are also listed in the *Format* popup under Globals.

The aspect ratio is the commonly held ratio. It is also goes in the *viewerAspectRatio* parameter in Globals when you work with video formats to protect the fields. For cinema formats, put the *defaultAspect* into the *proxyRatio*. Otherwise, the *defaultAspect* is the value that goes in the *Format* entry under Globals. Enter "1/aspect ratio" in any text field to calculate this value.

| Format | width | height | Aspect | defaultAspect |
|---|---|---|---|---|
| NTSC D1 | 720 | 486 | 9 | 1.111 |
| NTSC HD | 720 | 486 | 1.2 | .8333 |
| NTSC MPEG2/DV | 720 | 480 | .9 | 1.111 |
| PAL D1 | 720 | 576 | 1.066 | .938 |
| PAL Square | 768 | 576 | 1 | 1 |
| Academy | 1828 | 1556 | 1 | 1 |
| Cinemascope | 1828 | 1556 | 2 | .5 |
| Full | 2048 | 1556 | 1 | 1 |
| 1.85 | 1828 | 1332 | 1 | 1 |
| 1080 HD | 1920 | 1080 | 1 | 1 |
| 720 HD | 1280 | 720 | 1 | 1 |
| 720 HD Anamorphic | 960 | 720 | 1.3333 | 0.75 |

Nodes that help with resolution include: *Transform* – **Viewport**, **Crop** and **Window** (all change the border position), or **Zoom**, **Resize** or **Fit** (all scale the image resolution). You can also composite the image over a blank *Image* – **Color** node that contains the resolution you want.

## Anatomy of a Node

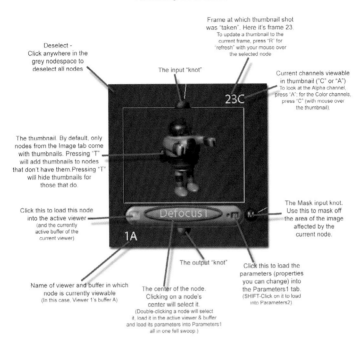

Frame at which thumbnail shot was "taken". Here it's frame 23. To update a thumbnail to the current frame, press "R" for "refresh" with your mouse over the selected node

Deselect - Click anywhere in the grey nodespace to deselect all nodes

The input "knot"

Current channels viewable in thumbnail ("C" or "A") To look at the Alpha channel, press "A"; for the Color channels, press "C" (with mouse over the thumbnail).

The thumbnail. By default, only nodes from the Image tab come with thumbnails. Pressing "T" will add thumbnails to nodes that don't have them. Pressing "T" will hide thumbnails for those that do.

Click this to load this node into the active viewer (and the currently active buffer of the current viewer)

The Mask input knot. Use this to mask off the area of the image affected by the current node.

The output "knot"

Click this to load the parameters (properties you can change) into the Parameters1 tab. (SHIFT-Click on it to load into Parameters2)

Name of viewer and buffer in which node is currently viewable (In this case, Viewer 1's buffer A)

The center of the node. Clicking on a node's center will select it. (Double-clicking a node will select it, load it in the active viewer & buffer and load its parameters into Parameters1 all in one fell swoop.)

## Fast Node Selection

Visual dyslexia being as ubiquitous as it is, you may find yourself searching in a daze for a specific node amid the kaleidoscope of icons in the tool tabs. Never fear: if you know the name of the node you're looking for, simply right-click on the tab heading (*Layer, Transform, Color*, etc.) and choose your node from the convenient alphabetical drop-down. You can even SHIFT-click, CTRL-click or CTRL-SHIFT click on these to access "branch", "replace" and "create" modes.

# The Node View

## Node View Shortcuts

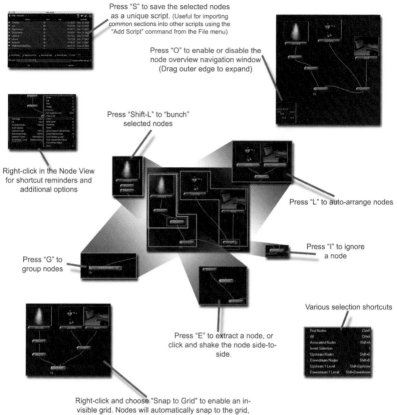

Press "S" to save the selected nodes as a unique script. (Useful for importing common sections into other scripts using the "Add Script" command from the File menu)

Press "O" to enable or disable the node overview navigation window (Drag outer edge to expand)

Press "Shift-L" to "bunch" selected nodes

Right-click in the Node View for shortcut reminders and additional options

Press "L" to auto-arrange nodes

Press "I" to ignore a node

Press "G" to group nodes

Various selection shortcuts

Press "E" to extract a node, or click and shake the node side-to-side.

Right-click and choose "Snap to Grid" to enable an invisible grid. Nodes will automatically snap to the grid, creating orderly alignment of the node tree. To change the size of the grid spacing, look in the *gridEnable* section of *guiSettings* under Globals

## Anatomy of the Enhanced Node View

showExpressionLinks lines
Indicates an expression link
between nodes. Arrow points
towards source.

showTimeDependency glows
Indicates whether a node contains
animated (i.e. keyframed) values.
FileIn nodes are all included in this
category

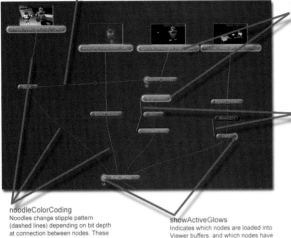

showConcatenationLinks lines
Indicates active concatenation
between adjacent nodes

noodleColorCoding
Noodles change stipple pattern
(dashed lines) depending on bit depth
at connection between nodes. These
can be changed in Globals.
Defaults:
8 bit - fine stippling
16 bit - medium stippling
32 bit - unbroken line

showActiveGlows
Indicates which nodes are loaded into
Viewer buffers, and which nodes have
parameters loaded into a Parameters
tab or Tweaker box.

`ctrl` `E`    Enable/disable Enhanced Node View

## The Favorites Preset System

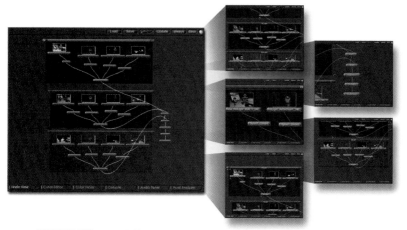

Shift + Function Key (F1-F5) (with mouse over desired screen quadrant)
Set current framing and state for chosen function key

Function Key (F1-F5) Only (with mouse over desired screen quadrant)
Recall saved framing (but not state)

Option + Function Key (F1-F5) (with mouse over desired screen quadrant)
Recall current framing and state (e.g. which node is in the loaded into the Viewer/which
node is loaded into Parameters1) for chosen function key

## The Mask Input

The mask input on the side of a node can appear quite confusing upon first encounter. It allows you to mix the output of the node back over the top of the input, based on the matte being fed into this side mask input. What it doesn't do is adjust the intensity of the applied operator (**Blur**, **Mult**, etc.). Rather, it is equivalent to applying the operator to the entire image and then mixing this output back into the original image based on the mask input matte (see image below). If the plan were, say, to adjust the intensity of a blur across an image based on a matte, an **IBlur** would be the node to use.

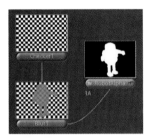 =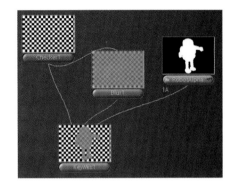

### Noodling

## Connecting Nodes With Noodles

Nodes are connected to each other by thin lines commonly known as "noodles". The noodles connect between small, round "knots"; knots at the top of a node are input knots, while those at the bottom are output knots. There are several ways to connect nodes together:

**Drag and release**    Drag a noodle from the output knot of one node to the input knot of the next, then release the mouse.

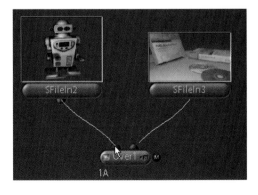

## The Node View

**Select and Shift-click**   Select the output node (by clicking its center), then Shift-click on the input knot of the "receiving" node to make the connection.

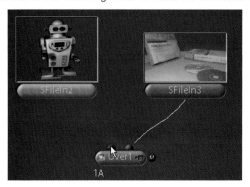

## Node Insertion Methods

When adding a new node to a Shake script, several methods are available. These methods and their keyboard shortcuts can be viewed by right-clicking on a node's button in the Tool Tabs.

**Insert**   Connects a node directly after the currently selected node. If the selected node already has multiple outputs, these outputs are reconnected to the output of the new node.

**Branch**   Connects a node after the currently selected node, but creates a separate noodle if other connections already exist. Existing noodles connecting to the selected node are unaffected.

**Replace**   Replaces the selected node with the new node, maintaining noodle connections where possible.

**Create**   Adds a node to the Node View with no connections, regardless of what node was already selected.

**Insert Multiple**   To attach the same kind of new node to several nodes at once, select the nodes in the Node view and then choose Insert Multiple.

**Drag Insert**   Simply drag a node over a noodle. When the input and output knots turn gold, release the mouse to insert.

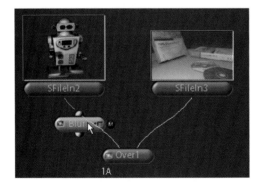

**Shake It Loose**   To extract a node from a noodle, simply shake it rapidly from side to side, or press the E key (the boring way).

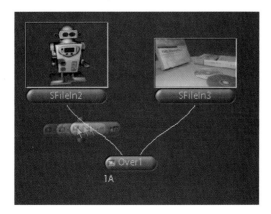

## Switching Noodles

If one of your noodles is in the wrong place, it's easy to fix. When you mouse over the *top* of a noodle, it turns **Yellow**. If you click and drag it, you can move it to another node's output knot and release it, linking it to the new node and breaking the connection to the old. When you mouse over the *bottom* of a noodle, it turns **Red**. If you click and drag it you can move it to another node's input knot and release it, linking it to the new node and breaking the connection to the old.

If you accidentally put two noodles the wrong way around (going into, say, an ***Over*** node), simply drag one of the noodles into the correct knot and Shake will automatically flip the other connection.

## Deleting Noodles

To delete a noodle, just mouse over until it turns red *or* yellow and press the FORWARD DELETE key (that's the small "DEL" key to the right of the main keyboard – FN-DELETE on a laptop).

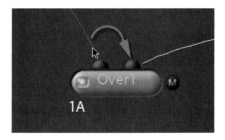

## Anatomy of the Viewer

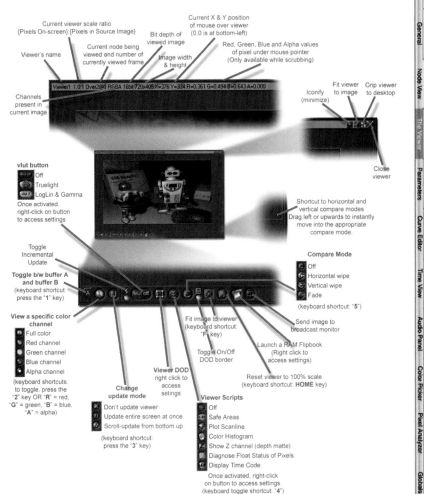

Current viewer scale ratio
{Pixels On-screen}:{Pixels in Source Image}

Current X & Y position
of mouse over viewer
(0,0 is at bottom-left)

Viewer's name

Current node being
viewed and number of
currently viewed frame

Bit depth of
viewed image

Image width
& height

Red, Green, Blue and Alpha values
of pixel under mouse pointer
(Only available while scrubbing)

Channels
present in
current image

`Viewer1: 1:0:1 Over2@1 RGBA 16bit 720x405 X=376 Y=334 R=0.361 G=0.494 B=0.643 A=0.000`

Iconify
(minimize)

Fit viewer
to image

Grip viewer
to desktop

**vlut button**

Off

Truelight

LogLin & Gamma

Once activated,
right-click on button
to access settings

Close
viewer

Shortcut to horizontal and
vertical compare modes
Drag left or upwards to instantly
move into the appropriate
compare mode.

Toggle
Incremental
Update

**Toggle b/w buffer A
and buffer B**
(keyboard shortcut:
press the "1" key)

**Compare Mode**

Off

Horizontal wipe

Vertical wipe

Fade

(keyboard shortcut: "5")

**View a specific color
channel**

Full color

Red channel

Green channel

Blue channel

Alpha channel

(keyboard shortcuts:
to toggle, press the
"2" key OR "R" = red,
"G" = green, "B" = blue,
"A" = alpha)

Fit image to viewer
(keyboard shortcut:
"F" key)

Toggle On/Off
DOD border

**Change
update mode**

Don't update viewer

Update entire screen at once

Scroll-update from bottom up

(keyboard shortcut:
press the "3" key)

**Viewer DOD**
right click to
access
setings

Send image to
broadcast monitor

Launch a RAM Flipbook
(Right click to
access settings)

Reset viewer to 100% scale
(keyboard shortcut: HOME key)

**Viewer Scripts**

Off

Safe Areas

Plot Scanline

Color Histogram

Show Z channel (depth matte)

Diagnose Float Status of Pixels

Display Time Code

Once activated, right-click
on button to access settings.
(keyboard toggle shortcut: "4")

General
Node View
The Viewer
Parameters
Curve Editor
Time View
Audio Panel
Color Picker
Pixel Analyzer
Globals

Interface
Image
Color
Filter
Key
Layer
Transform
Warp
Other
Scripting
Customizing
Keyboard

## The Viewer

### Anatomy of a RAM Flipbook

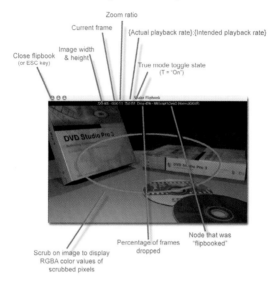

- Zoom ratio
- Current frame
- {Actual playback rate}:{Intended playback rate}
- Image width & height
- Close flipbook (or ESC key)
- True mode toggle state (T = "On")
- Node that was "flipbooked"
- Percentage of frames dropped
- Scrub on image to display RGBA color values of scrubbed pixels

### Flipbook Shortcuts

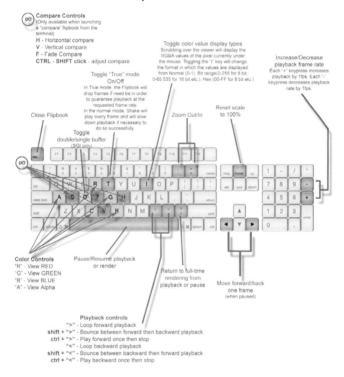

**Compare Controls**
(Only available when launching a "compare" flipbook from the terminal)
H - Horizontal compare
V - Vertical compare
F - Fade Compare
CTRL - SHIFT click - adjust compare

**Toggle color value display types**
Scrubbing over the viewer will display the RGBA values of the pixel currently under the mouse. Toggling the 'T' key will change the format in which the values are displayed, from Normal (0-1), Bit range(0-255 for 8 bit 0-65,535 for 16 bit etc.), Hex (00-FF for 8 bit etc.)

**Increase/Decrease playback frame rate**
Each '+' keypress increases playback by 1fps. Each '-' keypress decreases playback rate by 1fps.

**Toggle "True" mode On/Off**
In True mode, the Flipbook will drop frames if need be in order to guarantee playback at the requested frame rate. In the normal mode, Shake will play every frame and will slow down playback if necessary to do so successfully.

Zoom Out/In

Reset scale to 100%

Close Flipbook

**Toggle double/single buffer** (SGI only)

**Color Controls**
"R" - View RED
"G" - View GREEN
"B" - View BLUE
"A" - View Alpha

Pause/Resume playback or render

Return to full-time rendering from playback or pause

Move forward/back one frame (when paused)

**Playback controls**
">" - Loop forward playback
shift + ">" - Bounce between forward then backward playback
ctrl + ">" - Play forward once then stop
"<" - Loop backward playback
shift + "<" - Bounce between backward then forward playback
ctrl + "<" - Play backward once then stop

## Anatomy of Parameters

Choose channel
from mask input
source to be used
as grayscale

Click these LEDs to load
the corresponding node
into the Viewer

Manual text entry of
node connections
By giving short names to
commonly used nodes, these
nodes can be attached by
quickly typing that name into
one of these boxes. e.g.. "X"

Alternative Parameters tab
Shift-click on a node's parameters
widget to load into Parameters2.
Also useful for storing viewer script
controls

Launch HTML
documentation
on current
node

Animatable
parameter for
mask strength

Invert the mask

Clamp the mask
(Remove float values out-
side the range 0-1)

Enable/disable the mask

Ignore current node in tree
(same as pressing"I" in the node view)

Create chosen node type
and automatically attach to
node's mask input
(You may want to deactivate "en-
ableMask", below, prior to build-
ing a shape or Quickpainting)

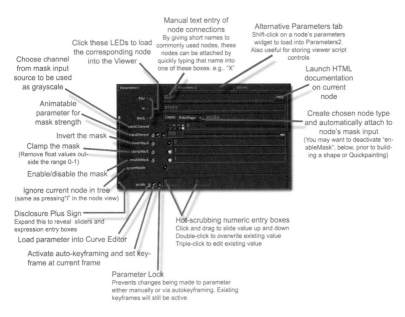

**Disclosure Plus Sign**
Expand this to reveal sliders and
expression entry boxes

Load parameter into Curve Editor

Activate auto-keyframing and set keyframe at current frame

Hot-scrubbing numeric entry boxes
Click and drag to slide value up and down
Double-click to overwrite existing value
Triple-click to edit existing value

Parameter Lock
Prevents changes being made to parameter
either manually or via autokeyframing. Existing
keyframes will still be active.

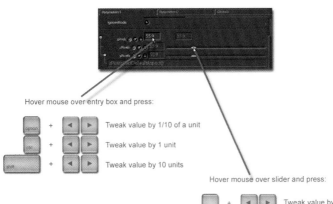

Hover mouse over entry box and press:

option + ◄ ► Tweak value by 1/10 of a unit

ctrl + ◄ ► Tweak value by 1 unit

shift + ◄ ► Tweak value by 10 units

Hover mouse over slider and press:

option + ◄ ► Tweak value by 1/100 of a unit

ctrl + ◄ ► Tweak value by 1/10 of a unit

shift + ◄ ► Tweak value by 1 unit

General | Interface | Image | Color | Filter | Key | Layer | Transform | Warp | Other | Scripting | Customizing | Keyboard

Node View | The Viewer | Parameters | Curve Editor | Time View | Audio Panel | Color Picker | Pixel Analyzer | Globals

## The Curve Editor

### Anatomy of the Curve Editor

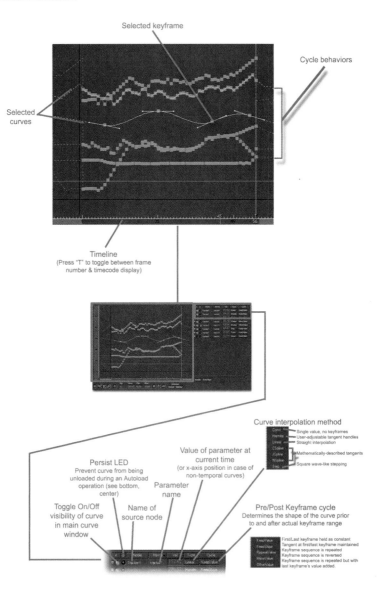

Selected keyframe

Cycle behaviors

Selected curves

Timeline
(Press "T" to toggle between frame
number & timecode display)

Curve interpolation method

Cant — Single value, no keyframes
Hermite — User-adjustable tangent handles
Linear — Straight interpolation
CSpline — Mathematically-described tangents
JSpline
NSpline
Step — Square wave-like stepping

Value of parameter at
current time
(or x-axis position in case of
non-temporal curves)

Persist LED
Prevent curve from being
unloaded during an Autoload
operation (see bottom,
center)

Parameter
name

Toggle On/Off
visibility of curve
in main curve
window

Name of
source node

Pre/Post Keyframe cycle
Determines the shape of the curve prior
to and after actual keyframe range

KeepValue — First/Last keyframe held as constant
KeepSlope — Tangent at first/last keyframe maintained
RepeatRate — Keyframe sequence is repeated
MirrorValue — Keyframe sequence is reversed
OffsetValue — Keyframe sequence is repeated but with
last keyframe's value added.

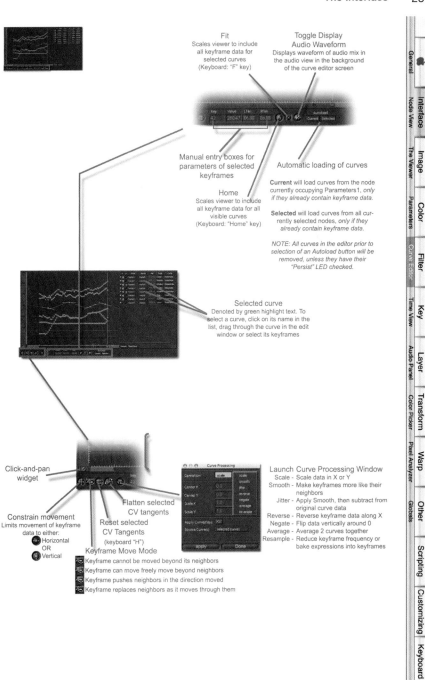

Fit
Scales viewer to include
all keyframe data for
selected curves
(Keyboard: "F" key)

Toggle Display
Audio Waveform
Displays waveform of audio mix in
the audio view in the background
of the curve editor screen

Manual entry boxes for
parameters of selected
keyframes

Automatic loading of curves

Home
Scales viewer to include
all keyframe data for all
visible curves
(Keyboard: "Home" key)

**Current** will load curves from the node
currently occupying Parameters1, *only
if they already contain keyframe data.*

**Selected** will load curves from all currently selected nodes, *only if they
already contain keyframe data.*

*NOTE: All curves in the editor prior to
selection of an Autoload button will be
removed, unless they have their
"Persist" LED checked.*

Selected curve
Denoted by green highlight text. To
select a curve, click on its name in the
list, drag through the curve in the edit
window or select its keyframes

Click-and-pan
widget

Constrain movement
Limits movement of keyframe
data to either:
● Horizontal
OR
● Vertical

Flatten selected
CV tangents

Reset selected
CV Tangents
(keyboard "H")

Keyframe Move Mode

Keyframe cannot be moved beyond its neighbors
Keyframe can move freely move beyond neighbors
Keyframe pushes neighbors in the direction moved
Keyframe replaces neighbors as it moves through them

Launch Curve Processing Window
Scale - Scale data in X or Y
Smooth - Make keyframes more like their
neighbors
Jitter - Apply Smooth, then subtract from
original curve data
Reverse - Reverse keyframe data along X
Negate - Flip data vertically around 0
Average - Average 2 curves together
Resample - Reduce keyframe frequency or
bake expressions into keyframes

General
Node View
The Viewer
Parameters
Curve Editor
Time View
Audio Panel
Color Picker
Pixel Analyzer
Globals

Interface
Image
Color
Filter
Key
Layer
Transform
Warp
Other
Scripting
Customizing
Keyboard

# The Curve Editor

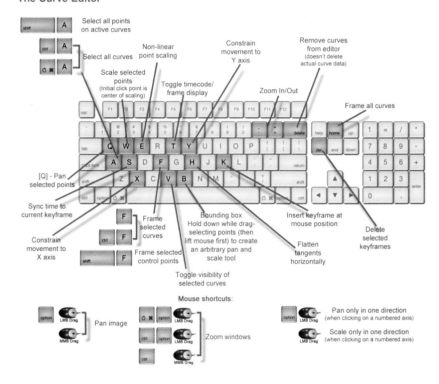

Select all points on active curves

Select all curves

Non-linear point scaling

Constrain movement to Y axis

Remove curves from editor (doesn't delete actual curve data)

Scale selected points (Initial click point is center of scaling)

Toggle timecode/ frame display

Zoom In/Out

Frame all curves

[Q] - Pan selected points

Sync time to current keyframe

Constrain movement to X axis

Frame selected curves

Frame selected control points

Bounding box Hold down while drag-selecting points (then lift mouse first) to create an arbitrary pan and scale tool

Toggle visibility of selected curves

Insert keyframe at mouse position

Flatten tangents horizontally

Delete selected keyframes

Mouse shortcuts:

Pan image

Zoom windows

Pan only in one direction (when clicking on a numbered axis)

Scale only in one direction (when clicking on a numbered axis)

## Anatomy of the Time View

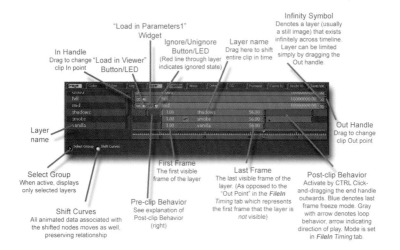

Infinity Symbol
Denotes a layer (usually a still image) that exists infinitely across timeline. Layer can be limited simply by dragging the Out handle.

"Load in Parameters1" Widget

In Handle
Drag to change "Load in Viewer" clip In point

Ignore/Unignore Button/LED
(Red line through layer indicates ignored state)

Layer name
Drag here to shift entire clip in time

Layer name

In Handle
Drag to change "Load in Viewer" clip In point Button/LED

Out Handle
Drag to change clip Out point

Select Group
When active, displays only selected layers

Shift Curves
All animated data associated with the shifted nodes moves as well, preserving relationship

First Frame
The first visible frame of the layer

Pre-clip Behavior
See explanation of Post-clip Behavior (right)

Last Frame
The last visible frame of the layer. (As opposed to the "Out Point" in the FileIn Timing tab which represents the first frame that the layer is not visible)

Post-clip Behavior
Activate by CTRL Click-and-dragging the end handle outwards. Blue denotes last frame freeze mode. Gray with arrow denotes loop behavior, arrow indicating direction of play. Mode is set in FileIn Timing tab.

## Anatomy of the Audio Panel

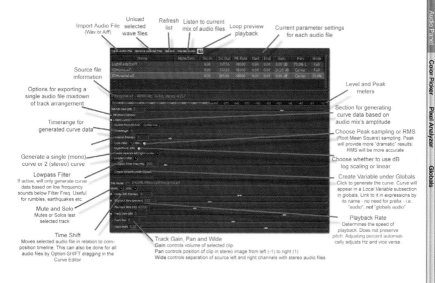

Import Audio File (Wav or Aiff)

Unload selected wave files

Refresh list

Listen to current mix of audio files

Loop preview playback

Current parameter settings for each audio file

Source file information

Level and Peak meters

Options for exporting a single audio file mixdown of track arrangement

Section for generating curve data based on audio mix's amplitude

Timerange for generated curve data

Choose Peak sampling or RMS (Root Mean Square) sampling. Peak will provide more "dramatic" results; RMS will be more accurate

Generate a single (mono) curve or 2 (stereo) curve

Choose whether to use dB log scaling or linear

Lowpass Filter
If active, will only generate curve data based on low frequency sounds below Filter Freq. Useful for rumbles, earthquakes etc

Create Variable under Globals
Click to generate the curve. Curve will appear in a Local Variable subsection in globals. Link to it in expressions by its name - no need for prefix - i.e. "audio", not 'globals audio'

Mute and Solo
Mutes or Solos last selected track

Playback Rate
Determines the speed of playback. Does not preserve pitch. Adjusting percent automatically adjusts Hz and vice versa

Time Shift
Moves selected audio file in relation to composition timeline. This can also be done for all audio files by Option-SHIFT dragging in the Curve Editor

Track Gain, Pan and Wide
Gain controls volume of selected clip
Pan controls position of clip in stereo image from left (-1) to right (1)
Wide controls separation of source left and right channels with stereo audio files

General
Node View
The Viewer
Parameters
Curve Editor
Time View
Audio Panel
Color Picker
Pixel Analyzer
Globals

Interface
Image
Color
Filter
Key
Layer
Transform
Warp
Other
Scripting
Customizing
Keyboard

# The Color Picker

## Anatomy of the Color Picker

**Sampling mode for Viewer scrub**
When scrubbing a color from the viewer, the final chosen value can be the last pixel selected (Current), the average of all pixels scrubbed (Average), the darkest of all scrubbed (Min) or the brightest (Max)

**Source buffer selector**
Use this to sample from the input of the node in the viewer instead of its output.

**Disable viewer sampling**

**HSV Color Wheel**
Standard Hue, Saturation and Value color wheel. Hue (the "essence of the color") is chosen via the angle around the circumference of the circle. Saturation (how "colorful" the choice is) is the distance from the center. At the center the chosen color is flat grey, at the edge it's entirely the chosen hue. Moving from the center to the edge, the color becomes less grey and more colorful. Value is the overall brightness of the color and is chosen via the slider at the base of the color wheel.

**Standard colors palette**
Click to choose a color for the active picker swatch, or click and drag to an inactive swatch.

**User preset palette**
Use these to store color presets, copy a color from one node to another or save favorite colors. (These save out with defaultui.h)

**Color Numeric Entry Boxes**
Manual entry of numeric color values. Boxes from left to right are for Red, Green, and Blue respectively. To manually type in a color value, double-click on the appropriate box and type the number (other entry boxes in Shake require only a single click). Click and drag left to right in the box to scrub through different color values. Hover the mouse at the base of a box to access a small slider for quick adjustments.

**For precision adjustments:**
Hold down the CTRL key while clicking and dragging in one of these boxes to get an extremely accurate adjustment. Once the adjustment exceeds one decimal place, the adjustment steps will revert to less precise, single-decimal-place values.

**Right-click color chooser**
Right-click over any swatch to access this instant palette. The top line contains a pure 0-code black, a pure mid-code grey and a pure 1-code white. The next line down supplies several RGB primary color combinations. Below is a full-spectrum color picker, and to the right is a grey scale gradient chooser.

**Standard color swatch**
To make active, left-click on the swatch. To deactivate, left-click again. An active swatch is indicated by a yellow outline around the swatch. When active, sampling colors by scrubbing over the Viewer or adjusting the HSV Color Wheel will automatically modify the swatch. When inactive, dragging from another swatch or palette can still change the color.

**Single master slider**
Large slider for adjusting a single color space property of your choice

**Individual red, green and blue entry boxes**
Use these to enter expressions to drive color based on another parameter, or to link, say, green to blue. SHIFT-click and drag the mouse from the label "blue" over the top of the label "green" and release.

**Master slider selector buttons**
Radio buttons for choosing which property the master slider is changing. These stand for

R - Modify Red
G - Modify Green
B - Modify Blue

H - Modify Hue
S - Modify Saturation
V - Modify Value

T - Modify Temperature (Red->Blue)
M - Modify Magenta content
V - Modify Value

The same letters operate as keyboard shortcuts: Hover the mouse over the swatch, hold down the "R" key, click and drag away from the swatch to adjust the red etc.

## Anatomy of the Pixel Analyzer

**Sampling mode for Viewer scrub**
When scrubbing a color from the viewer, the final chosen value can be the last pixel selected (Current), the average of all pixels scrubbed (Average), the darkest of all scrubbed (Min) or the brightest (Max)

**accumulate**
When activated, all mouse scrubs affect evaluation of Average, Minimum and Maximum. When deactivated, only last mouse scrub is used in evaluation.

**Sample area for Analysis**
Off - deactivated
Pixel - just sample pixels under mouse
Image - calculate Average, Min and Max from entire image

**reset**
Erases history of previous strokes when accumulate button is active

**Information Area**
Information about pixel currently under mouse pointer

**Min/max basis**
Method for determining what's considered minimum or maximum value

**Adjust Information Area Readings**
Toggles reading in information area between 0-255 (8 bit), 0-1023 (10 bit), 0-65535 (16 bit), 0-1 (normalized, bit depth independent) and Hexadecimal.

General | Interface | Image | Color | Filter | Key | Layer | Transform | Warp | Other | Scripting | Customizing | Keyboard

Node View | The Viewer | Parameters | Curve Editor | Time View | Audio Panel | Color Picker | Pixel Analyzer | Globals

# The Globals Tab

## Anatomy of the Globals Tab (top)

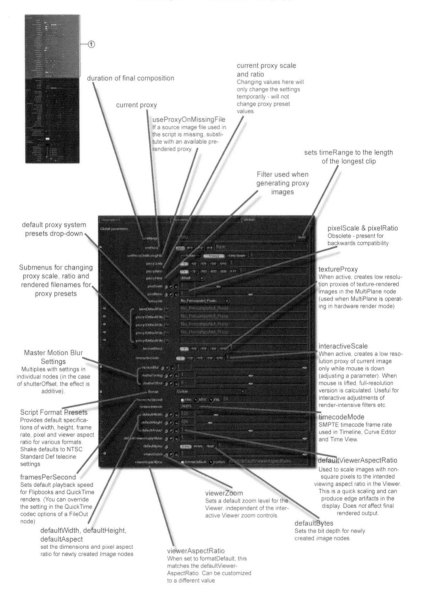

duration of final composition

current proxy scale and ratio
Changing values here will only change the settings temporarily - will not change proxy preset values.

current proxy

useProxyOnMissingFile
If a source image file used in the script is missing, substitute with an available pre-rendered proxy.

sets timeRange to the length of the longest clip

Filter used when generating proxy images

default proxy system presets drop-down

pixelScale & pixelRatio
Obsolete - present for backwards compatibility

Submenus for changing proxy scale, ratio and rendered filenames for proxy presets

textureProxy
When active, creates low resolution proxies of texture-rendered images in the MultiPlane node (used when MultiPlane is operating in hardware render mode)

Master Motion Blur Settings
Multiplies with settings in individual nodes (in the case of shutterOffset, the effect is additive).

interactiveScale
When active, creates a low resolution proxy of current image only while mouse is down (adjusting a parameter). When mouse is lifted, full-resolution version is calculated. Useful for interactive adjustments of render-intensive filters etc.

Script Format Presets
Provides default specifications of width, height, frame rate, pixel and viewer aspect ratio for various formats. Shake defaults to NTSC Standard Def telecine settings

timecodeMode
SMPTE timecode frame rate used in Timeline, Curve Editor and Time View.

framesPerSecond
Sets default playback speed for Flipbooks and QuickTime renders. (You can override the setting in the QuickTime codec options of a FileOut node)

defaultViewerAspectRatio
Used to scale images with non-square pixels to the intended viewing aspect ratio in the Viewer. This is a quick scaling and can produce edge artifacts in the display. Does not affect final rendered output.

viewerZoom
Sets a default zoom level for the Viewer, independent of the interactive Viewer zoom controls.

defaultWidth, defaultHeight, defaultAspect
set the dimensions and pixel aspect ratio for newly created Image nodes

defaultBytes
Sets the bit depth for newly created image nodes

viewerAspectRatio
When set to formatDefault, this matches the defaultViewer-AspectRatio. Can be customized to a different value

## Anatomy of the Globals Tab (middle)

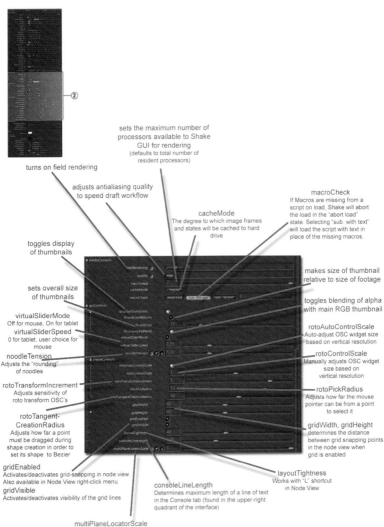

turns on field rendering

sets the maximum number of
processors available to Shake
GUI for rendering
(defaults to total number of
resident processors)

adjusts antialiasing quality
to speed draft workflow

**cacheMode**
The degree to which image frames
and states will be cached to hard
drive

**macroCheck**
If Macros are missing from a
script on load, Shake will abort
the load in the "abort load"
state. Selecting "sub. with text"
will load the script with text in
place of the missing macros.

toggles display
of thumbnails

makes size of thumbnail
relative to size of footage

sets overall size
of thumbnails

toggles blending of alpha
with main RGB thumbnail

**virtualSliderMode**
Off for mouse, On for tablet

**rotoAutoControlScale**
Auto-adjust OSC widget size
based on vertical resolution

**virtualSliderSpeed**
0 for tablet, user choice for
mouse

**rotoControlScale**
Manually adjusts OSC widget
size based on
vertical resolution

**noodleTension**
Adjusts the "rounding"
of noodles

**rotoTransformIncrement**
Adjusts sensitivity of
roto transform OSC's

**rotoPickRadius**
Adjusts how far the mouse
pointer can be from a point
to select it

**rotoTangent-
CreationRadius**
Adjusts how far a point
must be dragged during
shape creation in order to
set its shape to Bezier

**gridWidth, gridHeight**
determines the distance
between grid snapping points
in the node view when
grid is enabled

**gridEnabled**
Activates/deactivates grid-snapping in node view.
Also available in Node View right-click menu.

**layoutTightness**
Works with "L" shortcut
in Node View

**gridVisible**
Activates/deactivates visibility of the grid lines

**consoleLineLength**
Determines maximum length of a line of text
in the Console tab (found in the upper-right
quadrant of the interface)

**multiPlaneLocatorScale**
Scales the depth of all MultiPlane nodes found in the comp.
For convenience during setup only - does not affect data.

General · Interface · Image · Color · Filter · Key · Layer · Transform · Warp · Other · Scripting · Customizing · Keyboard · Node View · The Viewer · Parameters · Curve Editor · Time View · Audio Panel · Color Picker · Pixel Analyzer · Globals

# The Globals Tab

## Anatomy of the Globals Tab (bottom)

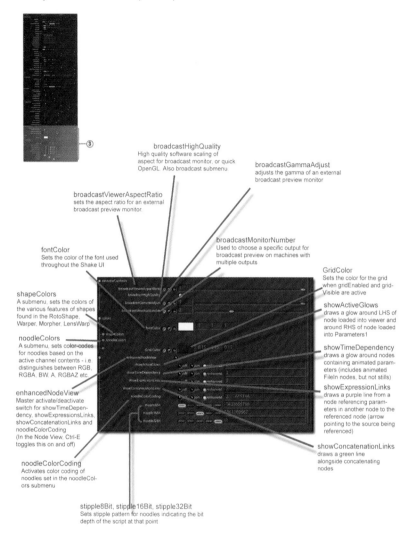

**③**

**broadcastHighQuality**
High quality software scaling of aspect for broadcast monitor, or quick OpenGL. Also broadcast submenu

**broadcastGammaAdjust**
adjusts the gamma of an external broadcast preview monitor

**broadcastViewerAspectRatio**
sets the aspect ratio for an external broadcast preview monitor.

**broadcastMonitorNumber**
Used to choose a specific output for broadcast preview on machines with multiple outputs

**fontColor**
Sets the color of the font used throughout the Shake UI

**GridColor**
Sets the color for the grid when gridEnabled and grid-Visible are active

**shapeColors**
A submenu, sets the colors of the various features of shapes found in the RotoShape, Warper, Morpher, LensWarp

**showActiveGlows**
draws a glow around LHS of node loaded into viewer and around RHS of node loaded into Parameters1

**noodleColors**
A submenu, sets color-codes for noodles based on the active channel contents - i.e. distinguishes between RGB, RGBA, BW, A, RGBAZ etc.

**showTimeDependency**
draws a glow around nodes containing animated parameters (includes animated FileIn nodes, but not stills)

**enhancedNodeView**
Master activate/deactivate switch for showTimeDependency, showExpressionsLinks, showConcatenationLinks and noodleColorCoding
(In the Node View, Ctrl-E toggles this on and off)

**showExpressionLinks**
draws a purple line from a node referencing parameters in another node to the referenced node (arrow pointing to the source being referenced)

**showConcatenationLinks**
draws a green line alongside concatenating nodes

**noodleColorCoding**
Activates color coding of noodles set in the noodleColors submenu

**stipple8Bit, stipple16Bit, stipple32Bit**
Sets stipple pattern for noodles indicating the bit depth of the script at that point

## The Image Tools

The Image tab contains the tools that actually generate an image. Nodes in other tabs manipulate images, but the Image tab actually creates the source images to be manipulated. The most common way to generate an image is to import footage from the hard drive via a *FileIn*. The exception here is the *FileOut*, which exports the final composite back to disk.

| | Checker | Generates a checkerboard image |
|---|---|---|
| | Color | Creates an image of a single pure color. Defaults to black. The default alpha value of the **Color** node is 1. |
| | ColorWheel | Use the ColorWheel to test color and keying functions |
| | FileIn | Imports single & sequential image sequences and QuickTime MOV's. This is where the following operations are performed: deinterlacing, 3:2 pull-down removal & addition, retiming, pre/post cycling behaviors and time shifting (in conjunction with the Time View). |
| | FileOut | Renders a composite out to disk. Can be attached anywhere in the composite tree to render out the state of the composite at that point. |
| | Grad | Creates a color image with 4 unique color graduations emanating from the 4 corners. |
| | QuickPaint | Use this node to fill in matte holes, remove tracking markers, clean up scratches, remove lines and other manual touch-ups. See page 36 for more information. |
| | QuickShape | The predecessor to the **RotoShape**. Included for legacy support. Still useful for attaching tracking markers to specific individual points via the text editor. |
| | Ramp | Creates a horizontal or vertical gradient with user-definable start and end colors. Default is Black – White. |
| | Rand | Generates color random noise. You can create interesting patterns by making small-resolution images (30x15 pixels) then blowing them up. |
| | RGrad | Generates a radial gradient with or without drop-off and with user-definable center and edge colors |
| | RotoShape | Primary rotoscoping tool in Shake. Also excellent for generating custom mattes. Features a soft edge variable at each individual shape point and motion blur generation. See page 38 for more information. |
| | Text | Generates anti-aliased text with basic kerning, movement and leading functionality. |

# FileIn

## Anatomy of a FileIn

The following items are available in the FileIn/FIleOut browser in addition to those found in the Open and Save script browser.

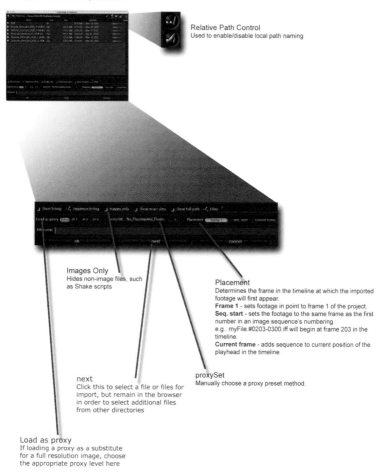

**Relative Path Control**
Used to enable/disable local path naming

**Images Only**
Hides non-image files, such as Shake scripts

**Placement**
Determines the frame in the timeline at which the imported footage will first appear.
**Frame 1** - sets footage in point to frame 1 of the project.
**Seq. start** - sets the footage to the same frame as the first number in an image sequence's numbering.
e.g.. myFile.#0203-0300.iff will begin at frame 203 in the timeline.
**Current frame** - adds sequence to current position of the playhead in the timeline

**next**
Click this to select a file or files for import, but remain in the browser in order to select additional files from other directories

**proxySet**
Manually choose a proxy preset method.

**Load as proxy**
If loading a proxy as a substitute for a full resolution image, choose the appropriate proxy level here

## Anatomy of the FileIn Source Tab

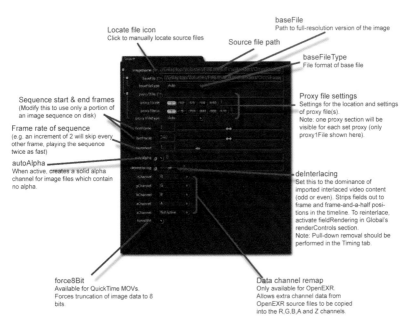

**baseFile**
Path to full-resolution version of the image

**Locate file icon**
Click to manually locate source files

Source file path

**baseFileType**
File format of base file

**Sequence start & end frames**
(Modify this to use only a portion of an image sequence on disk)

**Frame rate of sequence**
(e.g. an increment of 2 will skip every other frame, playing the sequence twice as fast)

**autoAlpha**
When active, creates a solid alpha channel for image files which contain no alpha.

**Proxy file settings**
Settings for the location and settings of proxy file(s).
Note: one proxy section will be visible for each set proxy (only proxy1File shown here).

**deInterlacing**
Set this to the dominance of imported interlaced video content (odd or even). Strips fields out to frame and frame-and-a-half positions in the timeline. To reinterlace, activate fieldRendering in Global's renderControls section.
Note: Pull-down removal should be performed in the Timing tab.

**force8Bit**
Available for QuickTime MOVs. Forces truncation of image data to 8 bits.

**Data channel remap**
Only available for OpenEXR.
Allows extra channel data from OpenEXR source files to be copied into the R,G,B,A and Z channels.

Interface | Image | Color | Filter | Key | Layer | Transform | Warp | Other | Scripting | Customizing | Keyboard

# FileIn

## Anatomy of the FileIn Timing Tab

**In and out modes**
Determines the behavior of footage extended beyond its 'natural' frame length. (Hold down the Ctrl key in the Time View while dragging the in or out handles of a clip to do so.) The options are:
[B]lack - displays black in R,G,B, and Alpha channels.
[F]reeze - holds on first/last frame
[M]irror - reverses sequence playback (e.g. for a 50 frame sequence playback would be ...48,49,50,49,48...)
[M]irror [I]nclusive - reverses sequence playback but repeats end frame (e.g. for a 50 frame sequence playback would be ...48,49,50,50,49,48...)

**timeShift**
Frame offset of sequence start from frame 1. e.g. a value of -5 indicates the sequence starts 5 frames before frame 1 (frame -4), while a value of 5 indicates the sequence commences 5 frames after frame 1 (frame 6).

**Sequence in and out points**
Affected by the changes to timeShift

**pulldown or pullup selection**

**field dominance of pulldown**

**firstFrame**
Set this to the order of the pulldown pattern at the first frame of the image sequence. A,B,C,D represent the four film frames of a traditional pulldown pattern.

**reTiming**
Sets the retiming mode. See below

---

**retimeMode**
Determines method used to create new frames.
Options are:
Blend - generates a new frame by blending (mixing) adjacent original frames).
Nearest - rounds down to nearest original frame - e.g. new frame for 5.7 would use frame 5 from original sequence.
Adaptive - uses high quality warping or optical flow

**new playback speed**
A value of 2 means twice as fast, 0.5 means half as fast

**Bit depth used for retiming**

**Method used for retiming**
Fast uses a mesh warp
Best calculates motion vectors

**Number of frames used in calculation of the blend**

**Weighting of adjacent frames during blending**
Weight of zero means all frames blended equally, higher weights cause frames closer to current frame to be favored in blending.

**Method used for deinterlacing**
Fast best for footage without moving subjects
Fast and good equivalent when working with standard definition footage

**Creates all new frames during retime**
No frames from the original sequence are re-used. All frames are generated by the retiming algorithm. Creates a softer image but protects against "pumping".

## Anatomy of the FileIn Timing Tab, cont.

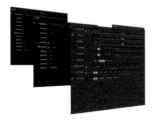

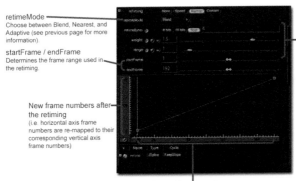

**retimeMode**
Choose between Blend, Nearest, and Adaptive (see previous page for more information).

**startFrame / endFrame**
Determines the frame range used in the retiming.

**retimeBytes, weight, and range**
See description on previous page

**New frame numbers after the retiming**
(i.e. horizontal axis frame numbers are re-mapped to their corresponding vertical axis frame numbers)

Original frame numbers

Useful for standards conversion
e.g. NTSC SD -> PAL HD

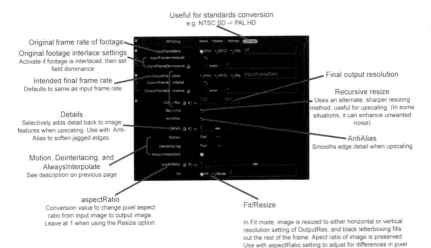

**Original frame rate of footage**

**Original footage interlace settings**
Activate if footage is interlaced, then set field dominance

**Intended final frame rate**
Defaults to same as input frame rate

**Details**
Selectively adds detail back to image features when upscaling. Use with Anti-Alias to soften jagged edges.

**Motion, Deinterlacing, and AlwaysInterpolate**
See description on previous page

**Final output resolution**

**Recursive resize**
Uses an alternate, sharper resizing method, useful for upscaling. (In some situations, it can enhance unwanted noise)

**AntiAlias**
Smooths edge detail when upscaling

**aspectRatio**
Conversion value to change pixel aspect ratio from input image to output image. Leave at 1 when using the Resize option.

**Fit/Resize**

In Fit mode, image is resized to either horizontal or vertical resolution setting of OutputRes, and black letterboxing fills out the rest of the frame. Apect ratio of image is preserved. Use with aspectRatio setting to adjust for differences in pixel apsect ratio between formats.

In Resize mode, image is stretched to match OutputRes. Aspect ratio is not maintained.

Interface | Image | Color | Filter | Key | Layer | Transform | Warp | Other | Scripting | Customizing | Keyboard

# QuickPaint

## Anatomy of QuickPaint's Toolbar (Onscreen Controls)

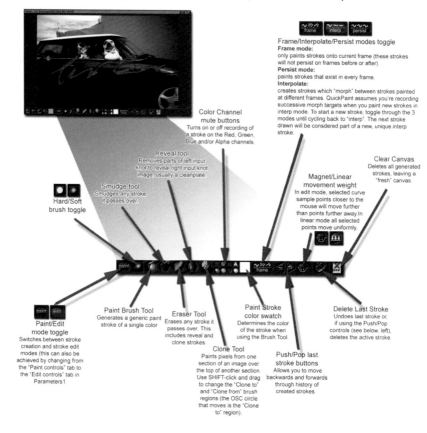

**Frame/Interpolate/Persist modes toggle**
**Frame mode:**
only paints strokes onto current frame (these strokes will not persist on frames before or after).
**Persist mode:**
paints strokes that exist in every frame.
**Interpolate:**
creates strokes which "morph" between strokes painted at different frames. QuickPaint assumes you're recording successive morph targets when you paint new strokes in interp mode. To start a new stroke, toggle through the 3 modes until cycling back to "interp". The next stroke drawn will be considered part of a new, unique interp stroke.

**Color Channel mute buttons**
Turns on or off recording of a stroke on the Red, Green, Blue and/or Alpha channels.

**Reveal tool**
Removes parts of left input knot to reveal right input knot image, usually a cleanplate.

**Smudge tool**
Smudges any stroke it passes over.

**Hard/Soft brush toggle**

**Clear Canvas**
Deletes all generated strokes, leaving a "fresh" canvas.

**Magnet/Linear movement weight**
In edit mode, selected curve sample points closer to the mouse will move further than points further away. In linear mode all selected points move uniformly.

**Paint/Edit mode toggle**
Switches between stroke creation and stroke edit modes (this can also be achieved by changing from the "Paint controls" tab to the "Edit controls" tab in Parameters1

**Paint Brush Tool**
Generates a generic paint stroke of a single color

**Eraser Tool**
Erases any stroke it passes over. This includes reveal and clone strokes.

**Paint Stroke color swatch**
Determines the color of the stroke when using the Brush Tool.

**Clone Tool**
Paints pixels from one section of an image over the top of another section. Use SHIFT-click and drag to change the "Clone to" and "Clone from" brush regions (the OSC circle that moves is the "Clone to" region).

**Push/Pop last stroke buttons**
Allows you to move backwards and forwards through history of created strokes.

**Delete Last Stroke**
Undoes last stroke or, if using the Push/Pop controls (see below, left), deletes the active stroke.

## Stroke Anatomy

**"Clone from" Area Indicator Circle**
When in Clone mode, this circle indicates which part of the image will be copied into the "Clone to" area.

**"Clone to" Area Indicator Circle**
When in Clone mode, this circle indicates where the clone brush will be painted. To adjust the offset of the "Clone to" brush from the "Clone from" brush, hold down the SHIFT key and click and drag. The circle which moves during this process is the "Clone to" circle; the area which stays anchored is the "Clone from" circle.
NOTE: Make sure you lift the SHIFT key up before releasing the mouse from this operation or you will automatically create a single "dot" of clone paint at the current position of the "Clone to" circle.

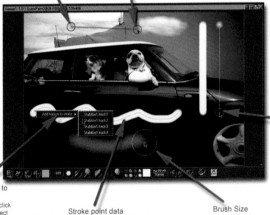

**Straight Line Draw Mode**
To draw a straight line, hold down the SHIFT key, then click at the intended start of the line. *With the SHIFT key still held down,* click again at the chosen end point of the line. For continuous connected straight lines, continue to click in the screen with the SHIFT key held down.

**Attach a tracker to a stroke**
In edit mode, right-click on a stroke and select a track from any tracking node (MatchMove Stabilize or Tracker) to attach. Once attached, the movement can be baked into the stroke by right-clicking again.

**Stroke point data**
When in edit mode, clicking on a stroke will display a fine outline at the center of the stroke. This is the point data for the stroke. You can drag-select through several points then click and drag them to reposition (or just click and drag a single point).

**Brush Size Indicator Circle**
To resize a brush, simply CTRL-Click and drag in the viewer.

Interface

Image

Color

Filter

Key

Layer

Transform

Warp

Other

Scripting

Customizing

Keyboard

# RotoShape

## Anatomy of RotoShape's On Screen Controls

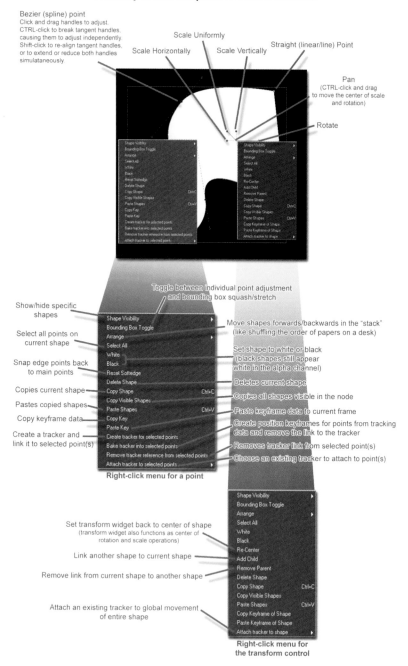

**Bezier (spline) point**
Click and drag handles to adjust.
CTRL-click to break tangent handles,
causing them to adjust independently.
Shift-click to re-align tangent handles,
or to extend or reduce both handles
simultaneously.

Scale Uniformly

Scale Horizontally     Scale Vertically

**Straight (linear/line) Point**

**Pan**
(CTRL-click and drag
to move the center of scale
and rotation)

Rotate

Toggle between individual point adjustment
and bounding box squash/stretch

Show/hide specific shapes

Select all points on current shape

Snap edge points back to main points

Copies current shape

Pastes copied shapes

Copy keyframe data

Create a tracker and link it to selected point(s)

Move shapes forwards/backwards in the "stack"
(like shuffling the order of papers on a desk)

Set shape to white or black
(black shapes still appear
white in the alpha channel)

Deletes current shape

Copies all shapes visible in the node

Paste keyframe data to current frame

Create position keyframes for points from tracking
data and remove the link to the tracker

Removes tracker link from selected point(s)

Choose an existing tracker to attach to point(s)

**Right-click menu for a point**

Set transform widget back to center of shape
(transform widget also functions as center of
rotation and scale operations)

Link another shape to current shape

Remove link from current shape to another shape

Attach an existing tracker to global movement
of entire shape

**Right-click menu for
the transform control**

## Anatomy of RotoShape's Viewer Buttons

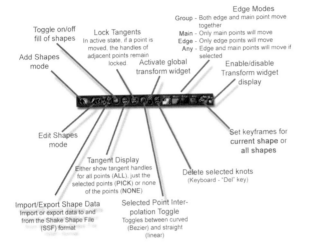

**Toggle on/off fill of shapes**

**Lock Tangents**
In active state, if a point is moved, the handles of adjacent points remain locked

**Add Shapes mode**

**Activate global transform widget**

**Edge Modes**
Group - Both edge and main point move together
Main - Only main points will move
Edge - Only edge points will move
Any - Edge and main points will move if selected

**Enable/disable Transform widget display**

**Edit Shapes mode**

**Set keyframes for current shape** or **all shapes**

**Tangent Display**
Either show tangent handles for all points (ALL), just the selected points (PICK) or none of the points (NONE)

**Delete selected knots**
(Keyboard - "Del" key)

**Import/Export Shape Data**
Import or export data to and from the Shake Shape File (SSF) format

**Selected Point Interpolation Toggle**
Toggles between curved (Bezier) and straight (linear)

Interface
Image
Color
Filter
Key
Layer
Transform
Warp
Other
Scripting
Customizing
Keyboard

## The Add Operator

Color operators can be broken down loosely into four groups: the Add, Mult, Gamma, and Lookup Operators. In addition, there are other color correctors, complex correctors, and utility correctors.

### The Add Operator

| | Add |
|---|---|
| **Function:** | Use to add or subtract numeric values from the pixels in the RGBA or Z channels of an image. |
| **Effect:** | *Mathematically*, contrast relationships between pixels are preserved; *perceptually*, contrast in the image changes due to the human eye's nonlinear scaling of brightness information. |
| **Uses:** | Commonly used to:<br>1. Adjust the "exposure" level of an image<br>2. Localized tasks, such as spill suppression (using the mask input to localize the areas of the image corrected). |
| **Premultiplication:** | Cannot be used with premultiplied images |
| **Concatenation:** | Yes |

### Case Study: The effects of an Add operator

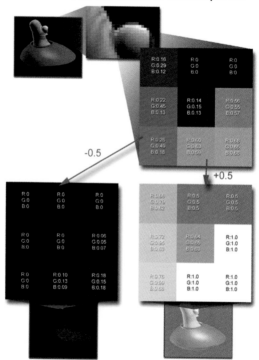

**The Mult Operators**

| | Mult |
|---|---|
| | |
| **Function:** | Use to multiply a numeric value from the pixels in the RGBA or Z channels of an image |
| **Effect:** | Though mathematically it adjusts the contrast relationship of the pixels in an image, *perceptually* it appears to brighten or darken the image. |
| **Uses:** | Commonly used to:<br>1. Brighten or darken an image<br>2. "Colorize" an image |
| **Premultiplication:** | A premultiplied image may endure subtle changes, though at larger values will visibly damage image edges. |
| **Concatenation:** | Yes |

| | Brightness |
|---|---|
| | |
| **Function:** | Mathematically identical to *Mult* (above), except that interface provides a single slider to uniformly adjust RGB channels (A and Z channels are unaffected) |
| **Effect:** | The same as *Mult* (above). |
| **Uses:** | Commonly used to brighten or darken an image. |
| **Premultiplication:** | The same as *Mult* (above) |
| **Concatenation:** | Yes |

| | Fade |
|---|---|
| | |
| **Function:** | Mathematically identical to a *Mult* (above), except that it provides a single slider to uniformly adjust RGBA channels (Z channel is unaffected) |
| **Effect:** | Fades an image from its default opacity to 100% transparent at a value of 0. |
| **Uses:** | Used to fade premultiplied images. |
| **Premultiplication:** | Safe to use on premultiplied images, since the alpha is scaled with the RGB channels. |
| **Concatenation:** | Yes |

Interface · Image · Color · Filter · Key · Layer · Transform · Warp · Other · Scripting · Customizing · Keyboard

## Case Study: The effects of a Mult operator

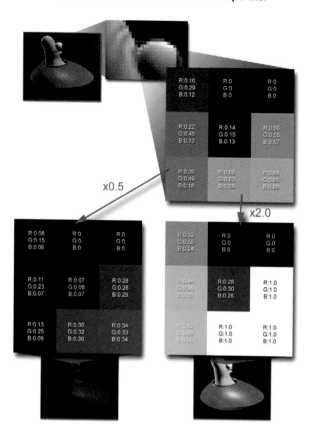

## The Gamma Operator

| | Gamma |
|---|---|
| **Function:** | Adjusts the contrast of an image using a gamma curve. |
| **Effect:** | *Mathematically*, raises input pixel values to the power of the inverse of the gamma value. *Perceptually*, adjusts the contrast of the image midrange. |
| **Uses:** | Commonly used to:<br>1. Adjust the contrast of an image without modifying the black and white points (regardless of the gamma value, pixels with values of 0 or 1 remain at 0 and 1 respectively). Mimics the response of the human eye, so is useful for making *perceptually* pleasing contrast changes.<br>2. Change gamma bias of images derived from different media, e.g. video content. |
| **Premultiplication:** | A premultiplied image may endure subtle changes, though at larger values will visibly damage image edges. |
| **Concatenation:** | Yes |

## The Lookup Operators

| | Lookup |
|---|---|
| **Function:** | Creates custom color curves based on mathematical expressions or user-defined keyframes |
| **Effect:** | A universal color correction tool |
| **Uses:** | Lookup can be used to mimic most of the other color correctors by drawing custom curves. It's most commonly used to:<br>1. Make color corrections to a specific area of brightness in an image, e.g. only the brightest pixels.<br>2. Correct an image based on an expression, e.g., "x*2" is equivalent to a *Mult* of 2. In many cases this is as flexible as *ColorX* and usually faster, due to scanline rendering rather than *ColorX*'s per-pixel calculations. |
| **Premultiplication:** | In the majority of cases, premultiplied images will be adversely affected |
| **Concatenation:** | Yes |

Interface  Image  Color  Filter  Key  Layer  Transform  Warp  Other  Scripting  Customizing  Keyboard

# The Lookup Operators

| | | |
|---|---|---|
| **LookupFile** | | **LookupFile** |
| | Function: | Creates custom color curves based on a lookup table inside an imported text file. |
| | Effect: | A universal color correction tool |
| | Uses: | LookupFile can be used with tables generated in other applications. Interpolation between points is linear, so it is generally only useful when table contains dense data. |
| | Premultiplication: | In the majority of cases, premultiplied images will be adversely affected |
| | Concatenation: | Yes |
| **LookupHLS** | | **LookupHLS** |
| | Function: | Identical to *Lookup* (above), except that it works in *Hue*, *Saturation* and *Luminance* (weighted luminance) space. |
| | Effect: | A universal color correction tool |
| | Uses: | See *Lookup* above. |
| | Premultiplication: | In the majority of cases, premultiplied images will be adversely affected |
| | Concatenation: | No |
| **LookupHSV** | | **LookupHSV** |
| | Function: | Identical to *Lookup* (above), except that it works in *Hue*, *Saturation* and *Value* (non-weighted luminance) space. |
| | Effect: | A universal color correction tool |
| | Uses: | See *Lookup* above. |
| | Premultiplication: | In the majority of cases, premultiplied images will be adversely affected |
| | Concatenation: | Only concatenates with other instances of itself or *AdjustHSV*. |

## Other Color Correctors

| | | |
|---|---|---|
| **AdjustHSV** | | |
| | **Function:** | Offsets Hue, Saturation and/or Value of an image by a defined amount |
| | **Effect:** | Changes a specific color within and image without tinting the entire images, as would be the case with a *Mult*. |
| | **Uses:** | Common Uses: |
| | | 1. Modify the color of a specific object in an image (often in conjunction with some kind of garbage matte in the mask input) |
| | | 2. Spill suppression (in conjunction with a spill matte in the mask input) |
| | **Premultiplication:** | If Value is affected on object edges, premultiplication will be an issue. |
| | **Concatenation:** | Only concatenates with other instances of itself or *LookupHSV*. |

| | | |
|---|---|---|
| **Clamp** | | |
| | **Function:** | Clips values to a specific range of values, e.g. 0-1 (the default) |
| | **Effect:** | Mathematically replaces numbers above the *Hi* value or below *Lo* value with the *Hi* and *Lo* values respectively. Perceptually, pixels outside this range look flat, or "overexposed". |
| | **Uses:** | Essential when working in float space. Any mattes generated in float space must be clamped between 0 and 1 (the default setting) before being applied in composite operations. |
| | **Premultiplication:** | Depends on the application. |
| | **Concatenation:** | Yes |

| | | |
|---|---|---|
| **Compress** | | |
| | **Function:** | Forces an image into a color contrast range, from the *Low* color through to the *High* color. |
| | **Effect:** | Perceptually, colorizes image into a particular color scheme. |
| | **Uses:** | Used for: |
| | | 1. Moving an image element into the general color tones of the background plate. |
| | | 2. Adding "atmosphere" to a shot, such as fog, smog or extreme radiosity from say, a sunset. |
| | **Premultiplication:** | Cannot be used with premultiplied images. |
| | **Concatenation:** | Only concatenates with self or *AdjustHSV*. |

Interface · Image · Color · Filter · Key · Layer · Transform · Warp · Other · Scripting · Customizing · Keyboard

| | | **ContrastLum** |
|---|---|---|
| ContrastLum | **Function:** | Adjusts contrast around a specific midpoint pixel value. |
| | **Effect:** | Perceptually, modifies the contrast of the images. Mathematically, it's the combination of an **Add** and a **Mult** (with the addition of a soft clip). |
| | **Uses:** | Used for adjusting contrast centered on a specific area of brightness. For example, if the darker regions of the image need to be emphasized, the contrast increase can be centered on these darker pixels. A soft clip smoothes the clipping points at 0 and 1. |
| | **Premultiplication:** | In most cases will adversely affect a premultiplied image. |
| | **Concatenation:** | No |

| | | **ContrastRGB** |
|---|---|---|
| ContrastRGB | **Function:** | Same as **ContrastLum** (above), but adjusts Red, Green and Blue channels separately. |
| | **Effect:** | See **ContrastLum**, above |
| | **Uses:** | See **ContrastLum**, above |
| | **Premultiplication:** | Cannot be used with premultiplied images. |
| | **Concatenation:** | Yes |

| | | **Expand** |
|---|---|---|
| Expand | **Function:** | Similar to **Compress**, expands arbitrary black and white points to absolute black (code value 0) and absolute white (code value 1). |
| | **Effect:** | Perceptually, colorizes image into a particular color scheme. |
| | **Uses:** | 1. Maximizing the contrast of an image by removing unneeded data from the darks and brights. 2. Neutralizing black and white points; using a PlotScanline, Red, Green and Blue can be equalized at the brightest and darkest points in the image to remove scene color biases. |
| | **Premultiplication:** | Cannot be used with premultiplied images. |
| | **Concatenation:** | Yes |

| | | **Invert** |
|---|---|---|
| Invert | **Function:** | Inverts an image – black to white, white to black etc. |
| | **Effect:** | Perceptually, creates a color negative of an image. Mathematically – Output = 1- Input |
| | **Uses:** | Most commonly used to invert a matte (note: most matte inputs have an invert toggle option built in). Useful for flexibility in operators like **Threshold**. |
| | **Premultiplication:** | Depends on the application |
| | **Concatenation:** | Yes. |

| | | **Monochrome** |
|---|---|---|
| | **Function:** | Generates a black and white version of an image via a weighted luminance |
| | **Effect:** | Perceptually creates a black and white version of an image, which is contrast-matched to the original color image. Rather than simply averaging red, green and blue together, the combining of the colors is averaged to take into account the sensitivity of the human eye to the three colors. This produces an image more compatible with the color image in terms of contrast than a simple mean average would. |
| | **Uses:** | Most commonly used to generate a black and white version of an image. The default weights – 59% green, 30% red and 11% blue – match YUV television standards. Can also be used to extract the luminance component from a video image without switching to YUV color space. Note: the default whites can be changed (for example, the node can be used to use only the red channel as the source of the black and white output image). |
| | **Premultiplication:** | Defaults will not damage a premultiplied image. |
| | **Concatenation:** | No |
| | | **Saturation** |
| | **Function:** | Increases/decreases saturation of the image |
| | **Effect:** | Perceptually, either makes the color look more intense or moves it towards gray. |
| | **Uses:** | Used to increase or decrease saturation |
| | **Premultiplication:** | Can damage edges of premultiplied images. |
| | **Concatenation:** | No |
| | | **Solarize** |
| | **Function:** | Partially inverts an image around a threshold |
| | **Effect:** | Perceptually, psychedelia. |
| | **Uses:** | 1. Think Beatles album covers 2. Isolating a specific range of pixels around a threshold in situations like special-purpose 3D matte passes. |
| | **Premultiplication:** | Depends on the application |
| | **Concatenation:** | Yes |
| | | **Threshold** |
| | **Function:** | Clips all pixels below a certain value to zero. |
| | **Effect:** | Isolates brighter parts of the image |
| | **Uses:** | 1. Isolate brighter image areas 2. With *crush* set to 1, generate pure 0,1 (black and white, no gray) mattes |
| | **Premultiplication:** | Will damage premultiplied images |
| | **Concatenation:** | Yes |

## Complex Correctors

| | ColorCorrect |
|---|---|
| 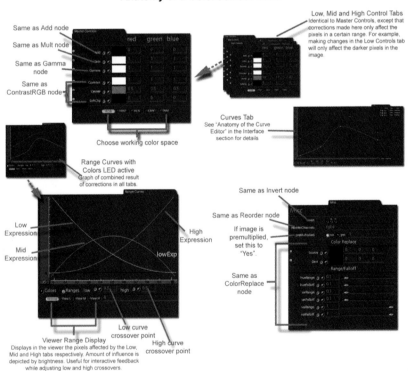 **C** Threshold | |
| **Function:** | A macro-corrector, containing many of the other discrete operators in a single interface (**Mult**, **Add**, **Gamma**, **ContrastRGB**, **ColorReplace**, **Invert**, **Reorder** and **Lookup**). Also breaks color correction into three brightness ranges: low, mid and high for localized color correction. |
| **Effect:** | Comprehensive color correction without needing to combine multiple nodes |
| **Uses:** | 1. Color correction in one place. This workflow is preferred by many users coming from other compositing platforms where this is modus operandi.<br>2. Performing color correction to localized sections of an image's brightness range. |
| **Premultiplication:** | Safe with premultiplied images; toggle the *preMultiplied LED* to "yes" in the *Misc* tab. |
| **Concatenation:** | Not with other color nodes. All internal operations do concatenate, however. |

### Anatomy of a ColorCorrect node

Low, Mid and High Control Tabs
Identical to Master Controls, except that corrections made here only affect the pixels in a certain range. For example, making changes in the Low Controls tab will only affect the darker pixels in the image.

Same as Add node

Same as Mult node

Same as Gamma node

Same as ContrastRGB node

Choose working color space

Curves Tab
See "Anatomy of the Curve Editor" in the Interface section for details

Range Curves with Colors LED active
Graph of combined result of corrections in all tabs.

Same as Invert node

Same as Reorder node

Low Expression

Mid Expression

High Expression

If image is premultiplied, set this to "Yes".

lowExp

Same as ColorReplace node

Low curve crossover point

High curve crossover point

Viewer Range Display
Displays in the viewer the pixels affected by the Low, Mid and High tabs respectively. Amount of influence is depicted by brightness. Useful for interactive feedback while adjusting low and high crossovers.

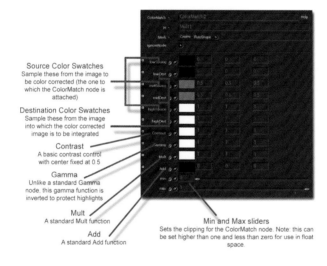

| | | ColorMatch |
|---|---|---|
| | **Function:** | Used to procedurally match a composite element into the color space of a background plate. |
| | **Effect:** | Using a look-up curve, shifts colors in the corrected element towards the equivalent colors in the background plate (e.g. makes the color and brightness of the darkest parts of the corrected image match the darkest parts of the background image). Similar mathematically to **Lookup**, but uses special algorithms to avoid solarization. |
| | **Uses:** | Very effective in matching composite elements filmed under different lighting conditions. Very important: requires intrinsically black/mid-gray/white scene elements to correctly match color spaces. E.g. A gray sweater in a foreground composite element could be matched to a gray trashcan in the background plate, *but only if the trashcan is truly gray*. If the trashcan is actually intrinsically green and only looks gray due to the cast of the scene lighting, using it as the mid destination color will yield false results. |
| | **Premultiplication:** | Cannot be used with premultiplied images |
| | **Concatenation:** | Yes |

## Anatomy of a ColorMatch Node

**Source Color Swatches**
Sample these from the image to be color corrected (the one to which the ColorMatch node is attached)

**Destination Color Swatches**
Sample these from the image into which the color corrected image is to be integrated

**Contrast**
A basic contrast control with center fixed at 0.5

**Gamma**
Unlike a standard Gamma node, this gamma function is inverted to protect highlights

**Mult**
A standard Mult function

**Add**
A standard Add function

**Min and Max sliders**
Sets the clipping for the ColorMatch node. Note: this can be set higher than one and less than zero for use in float space.

## Complex Correctors

| | | ColorReplace |
|---|---|---|
| ![ColorReplace] | **Function:** | Used to isolate a color based on Hue, Saturation and Value, then replace with a new color. Can also be used to generate a chroma key matte by selecting the "Affect alpha" option. |
| | **Effect:** | Changes certain colors in an image from a selected source color to a chosen destination color |
| | **Uses:** | 1. Color replacement (obviously) 2. Localized spill suppression. Useful for removing stubborn areas of spill that aren't removed by other methods. First, sample the problem pixels as the Source Color, and then reduce the problem color (say, blue for a bluescreen) in the Replace Color swatch. Increase the other colors (say, red and green) to compensate for reduction in brightness. |
| | **Premultiplication:** | Effect on premultiplied images depends on the severity of the color correction |
| | **Concatenation:** | No |

### Anatomy of a ColorReplace Node

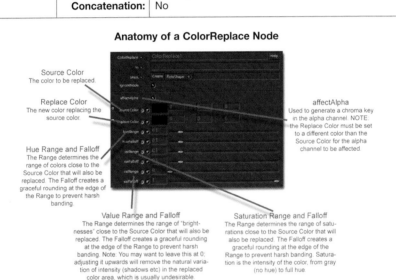

**Source Color**
The color to be replaced.

**Replace Color**
The new color replacing the source color.

**Hue Range and Falloff**
The Range determines the range of colors close to the Source Color that will also be replaced. The Falloff creates a graceful rounding at the edge of the Range to prevent harsh banding.

**affectAlpha**
Used to generate a chroma key in the alpha channel. NOTE: the Replace Color must be set to a different color than the Source Color for the alpha channel to be affected.

**Value Range and Falloff**
The Range determines the range of "brightnesses" close to the Source Color that will also be replaced. The Falloff creates a graceful rounding at the edge of the Range to prevent harsh banding. Note: You may want to leave this at 0; adjusting it upwards will remove the natural variation of intensity (shadows etc) in the replaced color area, which is usually undesirable.

**Saturation Range and Falloff**
The Range determines the range of saturations close to the Source Color that will also be replaced. The Falloff creates a graceful rounding at the edge of the Range to prevent harsh banding. Saturation is the intensity of the color, from gray (no hue) to full hue.

| | | HueCurves |
|---|---|---|
| 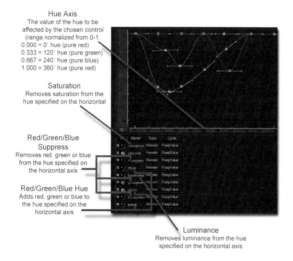 HueCurves | **Function:** | Performs color corrections to certain hues of an image. A curve editor determines which hues are affected. Think graphic equalizer for color instead of sound. |
| | **Effect:** | Perceptually increases or decreases brightness, contrast and saturation of specific colors in an image using Add, Contrast and Saturation operators on specific hues. |
| | **Uses:** | 1. Spill suppression of specific hues 2. Color-correction of specific hues 3. Returning foreground elements (clothing etc.) to appropriate colors after despill, preserving scene continuity. |
| | **Premultiplication:** | Depends on application |
| | **Concatenation:** | No |

## Anatomy of a HueCurves Node

**Hue Axis**
The value of the hue to be affected by the chosen control (range normalized from 0-1)
0.000 = 0˚ hue (pure red)
0.333 = 120˚ hue (pure green)
0.667 = 240˚ hue (pure blue)
1.000 = 360˚ hue (pure red)

**Saturation**
Removes saturation from the hue specified on the horizontal

**Red/Green/Blue Suppress**
Removes red, green or blue from the hue specified on the horizontal axis

**Red/Green/Blue Hue**
Adds red, green or blue to the hue specified on the horizontal axis

**Luminance**
Removes luminance from the hue specified on the horizontal axis

Interface Image Color Filter Key Layer Transform Warp Other Scripting Customizing Keyboard

## Complex Correctors

|  | LogLin |
|---|---|
| **Function:** | Converts Cineon Log images to and from linear space |
| **Effect:** | Expands logarithmic data into linear space for compositing. Clips original values above and below a specified black and white point respectively (unless in float space). Includes offset command to compensate for exposure level of source footage. |
| **Uses:** | 1. To prepare Cineon film scans for compositing and color correction in Shake's linear space. |
|  | 2. To convert linear images to Cineon format (Lin to Log) in preparation for recording back to film. |
| **Premultiplication:** | Will damage a premultiplied image (rarely applicable – premultiplication is almost always done to linear images) |
| **Concatenation:** | Yes |

### Anatomy of a LogLin Node

**Conversion direction radio buttons**
Toggle to "lin to log" when converting back from linear space to logarithmic space (usually prior to a Cineon-formatted FileOut.) Make sure identical settings are used for the Log-Lin and Lin-Log converter if converting back to the idetnical color space. (Try CTRL-SHIFT-V pasting the original Log-Lin node to the end of the script, then changing only the conversion button. This will guarantee future updates to the original LogLin will be automatically modified in the 2nd LogLin converter as well.)

**Black and White Points**
(green and blue controls are available for individual control; by default they follow rBlack or rWhite)
Determines the 10 bit cineon code values at which clipping occurs. Pixels below the Black point are clipped to the Black point and pixels above the White point are clipped to the value of the White point. This is done to compensate for the 8-bit buffer limitation in a standard computer display system. The data is clipped to maintain a useful contrast range while compositing. Use float space to preserve values above or below these clipping points or set these to 0 and 1023 respectively, then use a VLUT to adjust the viewer.

**Red, Green and Blue Offset**
Used to compensate for various exposure levels. Adjust these if footage appears too dark or too bright after LogLin is applied. A code value change of 90 is equivalent to an exposure change of 1 F-stop.

**Negative Gamma**
This should remain at 0.6

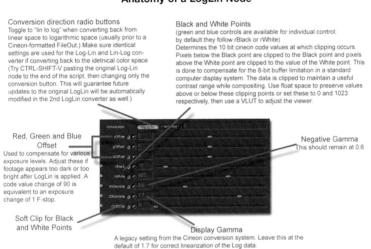

**Soft Clip for Black and White Points**

**Display Gamma**
A legacy setting from the Cineon conversion system. Leave this at the default of 1.7 for correct linearization of the Log data.

## Utility Correctors

| | | ColorSpace |
|---|---|---|
| **ColorSpace** | **Function:** | Converts from one colorspace to another, e.g. RGB - YUV |
| | **Effect:** | Replaces the Red, Green and Blue channels of the image with the contributing components of the new space. E.g. Going to YUV, the Y component is placed on the red channel, the U on the green channel and the V on the blue channel. |
| | **Uses:** | Used to move into and out of different color spaces. Very useful for switching to YUV colorspace in order to deal with video artifact such as 4:2:2, 4:1:1, 4:2:0 etc. |
| | **Premultiplication:** | Will not in itself damage premultiplied images |
| | **Concatenation:** | No |

| | | ColorX |
|---|---|---|
| **ColorX** | **Function:** | Applies user-defined arbitrary functions to the red, green, blue, alpha and Z channels of an image |
| | **Effect:** | Infinite number of possible corrections |
| | **Uses:** | Used to evaluate pixels and make decisions based on their color. Evaluates each pixel individually, making it processor intensive. Processes developed in ColorX can often be replicated with standard nodes like Threshold, improving render times. |
| | **Premultiplication:** | Depends on the application |
| | **Concatenation:** | No |

| | | MDiv and MMult |
|---|---|---|
| **MDiv** **MMult** | **Function:** | *MDiv* divides an image by its alpha. *MMult* premultiplies an image by its alpha |
| | **Effect:** | *MDiv* unpremultiplies an image; visually edges will appear aliased. *MMult* premultiplies the image; background area goes to black, edges are darkened in preparation for compositing into a background. Damage can occur to highlights in semi-transparent areas of the alpha. |
| | **Uses:** | Used to sandwich color corrections being applied to premultiplied images. The procedure is to apply an *MDiv* to unpremultiply the image, apply the color corrections, and then apply an *MMult* to repremultiply the image. |
| | **Premultiplication:** | N/A |
| | **Concatenation:** | No |

| | Reorder |
|---|---|
| **Function:** | A patchbay for color channels |
| **Effect:** | Re-arranges the R, G, B, A & Z channels in an image. So, the blue channel could be put into the red channel, the green into the alpha etc. |
| **Uses:** | Most common uses are:<br>1. To put one of the visible channels into the alpha channel (in cases such as a matte generated on the visible channels)<br>2. To make a grayscale image of a single channel by putting the same channel into red, green and blue. |
| **Premultiplication:** | In most cases this will affect a premultiplied image. |
| **Concatenation:** | No |

| | Set |
|---|---|
| **Function:** | Sets designate channels to single value |
| **Effect:** | Replaces the R, G, B, A and/or Z channels with a solid color. For example, the red channel could be set to 1, meaning that every pixel in the image will be fully red. |
| **Uses:** | Setting non-zero default values for pixels, such as 0.5 |
| **Premultiplication:** | Will usually damage premultiplied images |
| **Concatenation:** | Yes |

| | SetAlpha |
|---|---|
| **Function:** | Sets the alpha channel to a solid color |
| **Effect:** | Creates a pure alpha of a certain value and crops the infinite workspace to the dimensions of the image. It is a macro formed from a *Set* and a *Crop*. |
| **Uses:** | Used to prepare an image for finite transformations as a unique layer, since the entire layer's transparency can be set and the border is set at the edges of the current screen size. |
| **Premultiplication:** | Will not affect premultiplied state, but modifies alpha, removing the possibility of using *MDiv* and *MMult*. |
| **Concatenation:** | No |

|  | **SetBGColor** |
|---|---|
| **Function:** | Sets the color and alpha value for the area outside the DOD |
| **Effect:** | Sets the color of the background when a clip is expanded beyond the borders of its current Domain of Definition (DOD), either by a transform operator like Viewport or through a Layer operation |
| **Uses:** | Used to prevent edging when an image expands beyond its DOD. Examples: |
| | 1. A greenscreen may need to have a SetBGColor applied to make sure the area beyond the initial plate is keyed out if its borders are expanded prior to keying. |
| | 2. An image may need its alpha set to 1 to ensure that nothing is composited behind it when its borders are expanded. |
| **Premultiplication:** | Will usually damage premultiplied images |
| **Concatenation:** | No |

|  | **Truelight** |
|---|---|
| **Function:** | Applies a calibrated color correction |
| **Effect:** | Colors are shifted to match the gamut of a display profile |
| **Uses:** | Used to apply a color correction to simulate the look of output devices such as HD monitors and film projectors. Use in conjunction with the **TLCalibrate** in the **Other** tab. Also available as a VLUT. |
| **Premultiplication:** | N/A |
| **Concatenation:** | No |

|  | **VideoSafe** |
|---|---|
| **Function:** | Clips unsafe PAL or NTSC broadcast values |
| **Effect:** | Colors that are not "legal" for broadcast are scaled down into range. |
| **Uses:** | Used as a final step prior to rendering out files in preparation for broadcast. Not a replacement for Waveform/Vector scope adjustment, more a final safety measure. |
| **Premultiplication:** | N/A |
| **Concatenation:** | No |

Interface  Image  Color  Filter  Key  Layer  Transform  Warp  Other  Scripting  Customizing  Keyboard

## Bit Depth

Bit depth describes how many steps exist between black and white in your image. You typically use higher bit depths to remove banding artifacts. For film usage, you typically work in at least 16 bits per channel. In Shake, you can alter your bit depth at arbitrary points along the compositing tree.

**8 bits** per channel = 256 steps between black (0) and white (1).

**16 bits** per channel = 65,536 steps between black (0) and white (1).

**Float** per channel = Gazillions of steps between black (0) and white (1), but more importantly, you can retain values above 1 or below 0. This is particularly significant when dealing with Cineon files.

You can bump an image up to a higher bit depth when banding occurs, an artifact caused by too few steps between color levels. In this simple composite, a *Filter - **Blur*** is applied to some **Text**, and set to 600. Then, a *Color – **Brightness*** is applied and boosted to 20. The result at 8 bits has clear terracing.

Next, an *Other – **Bytes*** node is inserted between the **Text** and the **Blur**, and boosted to 16 bits. The result is now smooth.

Be sure to bring your bit depth back down if you do not need to remain at the higher bit depth.

## What is the Cineon Logarithmic Color Space?

The Cineon Logarithmic Color Space, or Log Space, is a method of handling color correction for film plates when scanning and recording. The Cineon file was specifically designed for film scans by Kodak. To accurately keep the color range of film, you need at least 14 bits. The Cineon file squeezes this information into 10 bits per channel by applying a special color correction. This color correction is called a logarithmic correction. Its basic curve is represented in the following illustration. The dotted line represents the input image.

Because the space is squeezed differently in the dark areas and the light areas, you cannot do standard color corrections or composites and expect the images to come out predictably when going back out to film. Therefore, you must correct the images back to standard linear space (what you deal with when working with digital image files). The conversion to linear space is shown in the following illustration. In this case, the dotted line represents the result image—the black bar is the correction curve.

clipping

## Log Space

So, the first step is to read in a Cineon file, and Shake automatically promotes it to 16 bits. Before you composite, attach a **Color – LogLin** operator to convert it to linear space. You then do your compositing. When done, apply a second **LogLin** operator, this time specifying *lin to log*. Finally, write your image out to a Cineon file with a **FileOut** node.

If you remain in linear space (for video output), this technique is fine. However, there is a problem when you convert from log space to linear, and then later re-convert back to log space to return to film. The standard log conversion formula as developed by Kodak has clipping built into it, which means bright highlights (think of bright shiny specular highlights on a new car), are lost when reconverting back to log.

The following graphs, with a **PlotScanline** on top of them, illustrate this clipping. The first graph is a straight ramp that represents a logarithmic scan:

When converted to linear space with a **LogLin** operator, some values get pushed above 1, nicely illustrated with the graph next:

Again, this solution is fine for linear space (broadcast, digital media). For film, however, apply a **LogLin** operator, and set *lin to log*. This should, mathematically, be the same as in the input ramp. However, this next graph shows lost data in both the high and low ends:

The solution is to boost your image to float bit depth before you convert to linear space (before the first **LogLin** operator). Because float can keep values above 1, your highlight information is retained, and ensures that your output image retains the same range as your input image.

You are not obliged to set your entire script in float. CG elements can be read in, modified, and composited at 8 or 16 bits per channel:

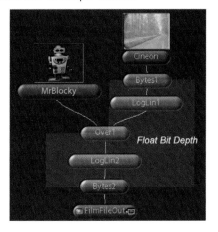

Keep in mind that jumping to float dramatically slows your processing, and creates much larger files on disk (if left at float bit depth).

The following formats support float bit depth: .iff, .mray, .rla, .rpf, .tif, and .exr. Cineon files (.cin) are always 10 bits.

The Filter tab contains the tools that modify an image using pixel-based evaluations. For example, at each pixel in an image a **Blur** examines the values of neighboring pixels, averages those values together, and replaces the original pixel with the new value. This makes each pixel more like its neighbors, *blurring* the image. Different weights can be given to the neighboring pixels' values, depending on their location relative to the pixel being evaluated. Different weighting systems are designated as matrices, known as *convolution kernels*. The majority of the filters in the Filter tab operate via convolution kernels.

| | | |
|---|---|---|
| ApplyFilter | **ApplyFilter** | Allows you to specify (if necessary) a different filter method for a horizontal and vertical blurring operation. The xScale and yScale control the blur amount. Slower than the **Blur** filter, it's included only for compatibility with other software packages. |
| Blur | **Blur** | A very efficient blur filter. Defaults to a Gaussian blur, but this can be changed for other filter types |
| Convolve | **Convolve** | Provides an interface for user-defined convolution kernels. These custom kernels must be defined and added via your nreal/include/startup folder as .h files. They'll then be available via **Convolve**'s drop-down menu. The standard Shake kernels are also available here. |
| Defocus | **Defocus** | Simulates defocused footage by blooming highlights as it blurs (unlike a regular blur which dulls and homogenizes the highlights). Various iris shapes can be selected (the default is circle) to match different camera aperture shapes. Iris selection also includes a fast Gaussian – this is useful as a draft setting for "roughing out" shots interactively. Note: Defocus is one of the most render intensive effects in Shake. |
| DilateErode | **DilateErode** | Expands (dilate) or shrinks (erodes) edges in the various channels (RGBA). The *soften* option is a falloff control rather than a genuine sub-pixel option. For sub-pixel dilate/erode of alpha channels, try the **KeyChew** macro in *Applications/ShakeX.XX/doc/html/cook/macros/* |
| EdgeDetect | **EdgeDetect** | Extracts edges of an image. **Note:** When generating edge mattes from an existing alpha matte, try combining two blurs of varying intensities (say, *xPixels* values of 3 and 5 respectively) with an **Xor** for a faster result than **EdgeDetect** (see right). |

| | Emboss | An engraving-type filter. To soften it, place a **Bytes** (promote to 16 bits) and a **Blur** before it. Also see **Relief** in *Applications/ShakeX.XX/doc/html/cook/macros/* |
|---|---|---|
| | FilmGrain | A powerful grain analysis and simulation system. Several common stock presets are also included. |
| | | To use the analysis tool, load the grain source clip into the Viewer. With the parameters for **FilmGrain** loaded, click and drag in the viewer to designate areas for analysis. Choose homogenous areas with little edge detail. Also try to choose mid-contrast and mid-brightness areas, preferably gray. Alternatively balance bright selection areas with darker ones. Note that sample boxes have a default minimum size that cannot be reduced. |
| | | To delete a sample box choose the "undo last region" button; |
| | | To delete all sample boxes, choose the "reset the regions" button. |
| | | When finished, choose the "analyze the grain" button. |
| | | You may need to make final adjustments to the intensity slider after analysis to deal with contrast inaccuracies. |
| | Grain | Inferior predecessor to **FilmGrain**. Its inclusion is primarily for legacy support |
| | IBlur, IDefocus, IDilateErode, IRBlur, ISharpen | Same operation as their "non-I" counterparts, but a matte on the second input determines the intensity of the effect across the image. **Note:** this is *not* the same thing as using the mask input on the regular, "non-I" node. See the mask input section on page 15. for more information. |
| | Median | Eats into one-pixel irregularies (by applying a 3 x 3 median convolution kernel). Useful for noise removal |

## The Filter Tools

| | PercentBlur | Identical in function to *Blur* (of which it's a macro), but offers blur parameter as a percentage of image width and height. |
|---|---|---|
| | Pixelize | Also known as a Mosaic filter, creates blocky pixels in place of source image. Think face occlusion in *Cops*. |
| | RBlur | A radial blur – blurs from a center point outward. Very useful for generating light rays effects etc. |
| | Sharpen | Increases contrast around edges in an image, creating the illusion of a sharper focus. |
| | ZBlur | Similar to *IBlur*, uses the Z depth of an image (if it has one) to control the blur. |
| | ZDefocus | Similar to *IDefocus*, uses the Z depth of an image (if it has one) to control the defocus. |

The Key tab contains the tools used to procedurally generate a matte, often referred to as a key (from video nomenclature). Looking for a Difference Key? Try **Common** in *Layer*.

| | | |
|---|---|---|
| ![ChromaKey] | **ChromaKey** | Generates a matte based on hue, saturation and value. **ColorReplace** can also be used with *affectAlpha* parameter enabled. Chroma keying is generally an inferior keying technique. For bluescreen and greenscreen work, use either **Keylight** or **Primatte**. |
| ![DepthKey] | **DepthKey** | Extracts a matte based on Z depth of an image |
| ![DepthSlice] | **DepthSlice** | Extracts a matte centered on a point in Z with drop-off in both directions |
| ![LumaKey] | **LumaKey** | A luminance-based keyer |
| ![Primatte] | **Primatte** | A third-party keyer from Photron. Uses a virtual 3D colorspace to generate a key. (See following page 65.) |
| ![SpillSuppress] | **SpillSuppress** | A basic spill suppression node. Works best on blue screens. Has compensation controls for loss of luminance during suppression |
| ![Keylight] | **Keylight** | A third-party keyer from CFC. Based on color difference keying principles. |

## Anatomy of Keylight

**screenColor Swatch**
Select this and scrub a part of the background to be keyed out. Try to choose a color that's in the middle (the median) of the luminance range of the key color.

**screenRange**
Increases the range of colors close to the screenColor that will be keyed out. Reduces garbage and holes in the matte at the expense of edge softness and detail. At a value of 0.3 all pixels in the matte are either 0 or 1 (black or white) with no gray pixels (i.e. no semi-transparency).

**fineControl section**
Controls for finessing the matte

**Shadow, Mid and Highlight Gain**
Adjusts opacity of dark, medium and bright pixels independently (as opposed to the screenRange). Can often be used to harden the matte in one pixel brightness range while preserving the soft edge in others. NOTE: can affect the color of the foreground, so be careful if using Keylight to composite as well as generating the matte.

**replaceColor**
The color substituted during spill suppression

**fgMult, fgGamma & saturation**
Standard Mult and Gamma color correctors if using Keylight for the final composite

**Plumbing Section**
Utility controls for choosing holdout and garbage matte color channels and temporarily ignoring the mattes (by turning off the appropriate LED)

Output Type
**comp:** Composites FG input over BG input, puts matte in alpha channel
**on Black:** Premultiplies the image, puts matter in alpha channel
**un-premult:** Outputs an unpremultiplied image, with spill suppression applied and matte in alpha channel
**status:** diagnostic output, indicating which pixels are background (black), spill suppressed (blue) or foreground (green, with brightness indicating opacity - dark = more opaque).

**fgBias**
Used to reduce spill on foreground. Note: also affects the opacity of the matte - may improve the key, or unnecessarily harden the edges. Useful for lighter regions of foreground, such a blonde hair in front of a bluescreen.
Tip: the default is 0.9,0.9,0.9. To save retyping this every time you make a change, click and drag the default swatch up into a custom palett swatch. Then drag back down from that swatc whenever you want to reset the fgBias

**Shadow, Mid and Highlight Balance**
Adjusts weighting of the colors being subtracte from the screenColor. Eg. if red is stronger tha green in the foreground of a bluescreen, adjust ing these sliders toward zero may produce a more solid foreground. Expressions set a default value for blue screen or green screen.

**midTonesAt**
Adjusts which pixel brightness values are affected by which of the shadow, mid and high light sliders in the fineControl section. i.e. it adjusts the crossover point of the 3 controls for Balance and Gain.

**colourSpace**
The color space of the source image. If film is still in log space, use log. Use video for footage originating in video format.

Interface | Image | Color | Filter | Key | Layer | Transform | Warp | Other | Scripting | Customizing | Keyboard

### To Key Bluescreens and Greenscreens with Keylight:

1. Apply **Keylight** to the bluescreen. Insert an optional background image into knot. An alternative is to set *output* to *onReplace*, and then change it later.
2. Select the *SreenColorScreenColor* color picker and select some blue area.
3. Open the *fine control* sub-tab and adjust *shadow*, *midtone* or *highlightGain* parameters, according to where your holes are in the matte.
4. If some areas go to pinkish purple (on bluescreens), try using the *fgBias* color picker to reselect some color. For example, if you have blond hair, you might pick the blond color. This will modify your mask as well as your color.
5. If you know you will do color corrections later on, set the *output* to *unPremult*.

6. To get your keys on multiple areas, combine them with **KeyMix** and **RotoShapes**.

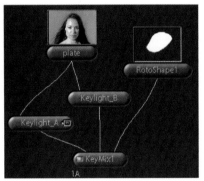

7. Use the *screenRange* parameter sparingly. You typically only use it on a node that is treated and fed into a second keying node as a holdout mask.

## Anatomy of Primatte

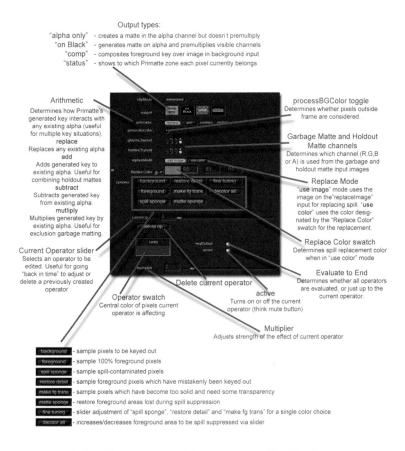

Output types:
- "alpha only" - creates a matte in the alpha channel but doesn't premultiply
- "on Black" - generates matte on alpha and premultiplies visible channels
- "comp" - composites foreground key over image in background input
- "status" - shows to which Primatte zone each pixel currently belongs

**Arithmetic**
Determines how Primatte's generated key interacts with any existing alpha (useful for multiple key situations).
**replace**
Replaces any existing alpha
**add**
Adds generated key to existing alpha. Useful for combining holdout mattes
**subtract**
Subtracts generated key from existing alpha.
**mutliply**
Multiplies generated key by existing alpha. Useful for exclusion garbage matting.

**Current Operator slider**
Selects an operator to be edited. Useful for going "back in time" to adjust or delete a previously created operator

**Operator swatch**
Central color of pixels current operator is affecting

**Delete current operator**

**active**
Turns on or off the current operator (think mute button)

**Multiplier**
Adjusts strength of the effect of current operator

**processBGColor toggle**
Determines whether pixels outside frame are considered.

**Garbage Matte and Holdout Matte channels**
Determines which channel (R,G,B or A) is used from the garbage and holdout matte input images

**Replace Mode**
"use image" mode uses the image on the "replaceImage" input for replacing spill. "use color" uses the color designated by the "Replace Color" swatch for the replacement.

**Replace Color swatch**
Determines spill replacement color when in "use color" mode

**Evaluate to End**
Determines whether all operators are evaluated, or just up to the current operator.

- **background** - sample pixels to be keyed out
- **foreground** - sample 100% foreground pixels
- **spill sponge** - sample spill-contaminated pixels
- **restore detail** - sample foreground pixels which have mistakenly been keyed out
- **make fg trans** - sample pixels which have become too solid and need some transparency
- **matte sponge** - restore foreground areas lost during spill suppression
- **fine tuning** - slider adjustment of "spill sponge", "restore detail" and "make fg trans" for a single color choice
- **decolor all** - increases/decreases foreground area to be spill suppressed via slider

## To Key Bluescreens and Greenscreens with Primatte:

1. Attach **Primatte** to bluescreen and scrub on a representative blue area.
2. Attach a temporary background for testing purposes. You typically want to composite later with the **Over** node.
3. Look at your alpha by typing A in the Viewer. If there are holes, click the *foreground* button and scrub it. For each holed area, select *foreground* again. The more strokes you do, the more blue will be introduced into the result. You may require a holdout matte, which is inserted into knot 4 on the top of the node.

4.  If there are badly keyed areas, use the *background* button. The more scrubs you apply, the crunchier your matte. You may require a garbage matte, which is inserted into knot 3 on the top of the node.

5.  Set your *output* to *comp* to test the result of the composition.

6.  If there are blue areas, apply a *finetuning* scrub on the spill areas.

7.  Once you have picked a color, you can adjust the sliders:

    **spillsponge slider:** Decreases the blue spill
    **fgTrans slider**: Adjusts the opacity of the less transparent areas
    **detailTrans slider**: Adjusts the opacity of the more transparent areas

8.  Background color for the *spillSponge* is from the background image (if there is one) or from the *replaceImage*, knot 6 on top.

9.  To make adjustments, use the *currentOp* slider to find your different functions. To re-scrub, click on the color picker and scrub.

10. The more *foreground/background* scrubs you do, the crunchier your key. This is bad.

**Basic Keying Survival Guide**

### Strategy 1: Concentrate on strengthening the mask

**Keylight** has great spill suppression and soft edges, so try to take advantage of this by letting it modify your RGB channels while you work on your mask. Typically, you pull two keys, a soft key in **Keylight**, and a second hard key (**Keylight** with a high *screenRange*, or lots of picks in **Primatte**) and feed the second key into **Keylight's** *holdoutMatte* input, knot 3. The second key may have negative *Filter – DilateErode* functions and **Blurs** applied. **IAdd**, **Inside**, **Outside** and **KeyMix** can also can help.

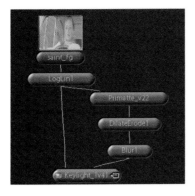

### Strategy 2: Work on the RGB separately from the Alpha

Keying is difficult, as is spill suppression. Why do both at the same time? Instead, work on your RGB separately from your alpha, and copy the result over with a *Layer – SwitchMatte*. This also allows you to work on your alpha at 8 bit and your RGB in float.

Useful spill suppression nodes:
- *Key – SpillSuppress*
- *Color – HueCurves*. Load the saturation curve into the Curve Editor and pull down the .66 (for bluescreens) or the .33 knot (for greenscreens).

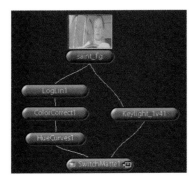

Interface  Image  Color  Filter  Key  Layer  Transform  Warp  Other  Scripting  Customizing  Keyboard

# The Layer Tools

The Layer tab contains the tools used to combine two or more layers to create a new, single composited image. This is how stuff gets glued together. The **Over** node and the **KeyMix** node are the most common nodes. Use the **Over** node when the matte used for the composite is embedded in the foreground alpha; use the **KeyMix** node when the image is not premultiplied and the matte is coming from a node separate from the foreground image.

| | | |
|---|---|---|
| AddMix | **AddMix** | Similar to an **Over**, but provides curves to adjust the edge transition from background to foreground. |
| AddText | **AddText** | Similar to *Text*, a simple method for adding text over an image. Useful for window burns etc. |
| Atop | **Atop** | A combination of **Inside** and **Over**, performs an **Over** only where alpha information exists in the background image. Good for putting things like smoke over CG characters |
| Common | **Common** | A difference extractor. |
| Constraint | **Constraint** | Can be used to compare two images and only pass through aspects that follow specific constraints. The two most commonly used are *Area of Influence (AOI)*, which allows you to draw a box to limit the images and *Threshold*, which passes only minor differences (or the opposite) through. |
| Copy | **Copy** | Copies the selected channels (R, G, B, A & Z) from the second image to the first. Unlike **SwitchMatte**, copying the alpha will not premultiply the image. |
| IAdd | **IAdd** | Adds the values of pixels in the left image to the values of corresponding pixels in the right image. The slider controls how much of the second image is added. Useful for combining light, as long as clipping doesn't occur (in which case try a **Screen**). **Note:** should *not* be used for combining mattes, as soft edge clipping will occur – use a **Max** or a **Screen** instead. |
| IDiv | **IDiv** | Divides the first image by the second. The slider controls the strength of the second image |
| IMult | **IMult** | Multiplies the values of pixels in the left image with the values of corresponding pixels in the right image. The slider controls the strength of the second image. |
| Inside | **Inside** | Keeps pixels in the first image only where there are non-black pixels in the alpha of the second image. **Very important**: also sets the DOD to that of the second image. |

| | Interlace | Interlaces two images together. Useful for older 3D renders where fields were rendered as separate files; standard deinterlacing/interlacing is handled in the *FileIn* node and *Globals > renderControls > fieldRendering* |
|---|---|---|
| | ISub | Subtracts the values of pixels in the second image away from the values of corresponding pixels in the first image. The slider controls how much of the second image is subtracted. Useful for combining garbage mattes etc. |
| | ISubA | Similar to *ISub*, but returns the absolute value of the result (i.e. any resulting negative values are returned as positive; in *ISub* these would be clipped to 0 in 8 bit or 16 bit space) |
| | KeyMix | Places the image on the second input over the image on the first input using one of the channels of the image on the third (key) input. Note: unlike all other nodes, the *background* is the first input and the *foreground* is the second input. The foreground image must be unpremultiplied |
| | LayerX | Composites two layers via user-defined mathematical expressions |
| | Max | The two input images are compared at each pixel location and the brightest pixel is used for the final output. |
| | Min | The two input images are compared at each pixel location and the darkest pixel is used for the final output. |
| | Mix | The equivalent of a video fade in a non-linear editor, the first input is cross-faded with the second via a mix slider |
| | MultiLayer | The heart of the Photoshop import engine, MultiLayer allows you to combine an unlimited number of layers together in one node. A "plus" sign on top of the node allows for the continued connection of more nodes. Opacity settings and layer functions (or transfer modes) can be set for each layer. Layers can also be reordered from within the *Parameters* window. Standard Photoshop transfer modes can be accessed here. (Using File > Import Photoshop File... generates a MultiLayer node to combine the various Photoshop layers.) |

Interface Image Color Filter Key Layer Transform Warp Other Scripting Customizing Keyboard

| | | |
|---|---|---|
| | **MultiPlane** | The 3D compositing node, MultiPlane allows you to composite multiple image planes in a virtual 3D space, then orient animate virtual cameras to render out a final 2D image. Point cloud data can be imported from 3D matchmovers via the alias .ma file format, along with the associated camera data. Image planes can be fixed to the point cloud data either with a single point positional lock, or with a 3 point planar lock. |
| | **Outside** | The opposite of *Inside,* this node cuts a hole in the first image wherever non-black pixels exist in the alpha channel of the second image. Does not affect the DOD. |
| | **Over** | The most common *Layer* operator, uses the foreground alpha to composite it over the background. Assumes that the image has been premultiplied, but there's a premultiply toggle in cases where it isn't |
| | **Screen** | Simulates a filmic blending by generating negatives of source clips (invert), multiplying them together, then creating a positive out of the result. Very useful for combining bright images, since pixels will tend closer to 1 (full brightness) but never clip. Not really compatible with float space unless source images are clamped. |
| | **SwitchMatte** | Takes any channel from the second input and places it in the alpha channel of the first. By default it also pre-multiplies the visible channels by the new alpha (can be turned off). |
| | **Under** | Know what an *Over* is? Same thing, just has the input order reversed for script tree layout and command line convenience. |
| | **Xor** | Confusing but remarkably useful, it returns whatever is mutually exclusive based on the alpha channels of both images. What does this mean? Wherever white bits of the alphas overlap, the resulting alpha will be black. Where they don't overlap, the alpha remains intact. See the **EdgeDetect** explanation in the *Filters* section for details on using Xor to generate an edge matte. |
| | **ZCompose** | Compares the Z depth of the two images and composites the pixel with the lowest value. **Note:** Z-compositing is fundamentally flawed; each pixel comes either from the foreground or background, so there's no blending of the soft edge. |

## Anatomy of a MultiPlane

**Right-click menu**
**First menu item (changes name depending on currently selected view)**
Sets the view displayed in the quadrant beneath the menu. Choose from
existing cameras, front, top, side and perspective views

**Plane Visibility**
Provides a checklist to show/hide all layers in the MultiPlane. Note: Hidden
layers will NOT render in final composite unless reactivated first.
**Current Object**
Provides a checklist to select a specific object or camera for editing. OSC's
will be visible for selected object (camera is selected in image below).
**Favorite Views**
Provides access to save and recall of favorite views (also accessible via
function keys F1 - F5)

Indicates the name of layer
currently under mouse pointer

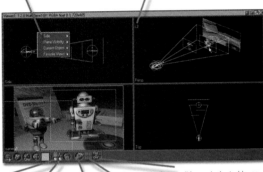

Keyframe all layers/selected layer

Activate/deactivate OSC's
for rotation adjustment

Show/hide point cloud

**Change viewer layouts**
Cycle between 1, 2, 3 and 4 quadrant layouts in Viewer by clicking
repeatedly on this button, or clicking and holding down mouse for
pop-up selection.

**Rendering mode**
Choose between Software, Hardware, or On release.
Software rendering is the most accurate, but slow to refresh.
Hardware takes advantage of graphics card OpenGL acceleration,
but may be less accurate, especially on high resolution layers.
On release will use Hardware while mouse is down, and Software
when mouse is released.
Regardless of selection here, final rendered output will be per-
formed at full quality. Hardware or On release modes are recom-
mended for interactive adjustment of controls.

Interface
Image
Color
Filter
Key
Layer
Transform
Warp
Other
Scripting
Customizing
Keyboard

# MultiPlane

## Anatomy of a MultiPlane (cont.)

Camera Frustrum
Rectangular end of pyramid projected from camera represents the final rendered frame of the camera.

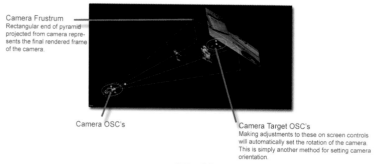

Camera OSC's

Camera Target OSC's
Making adjustments to these on screen controls will automatically set the rotation of the camera. This is simply another method for setting camera orientation.

Y Translation

Z Translation

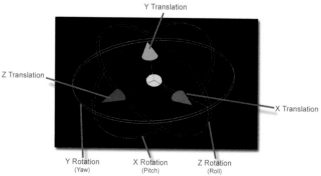

X Translation

Y Rotation
(Yaw)

X Rotation
(Pitch)

Z Rotation
(Roll)

Center (pivot point) controls
Hold down Control key while moving to adjust location

Local axis pan controls

Scale layer's plane uniformly

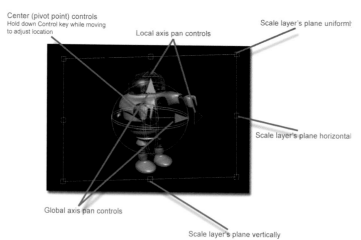

Scale layer's plane horizontal

Global axis pan controls

Scale layer's plane vertically

# Anatomy of the MultiPlane Image Tab

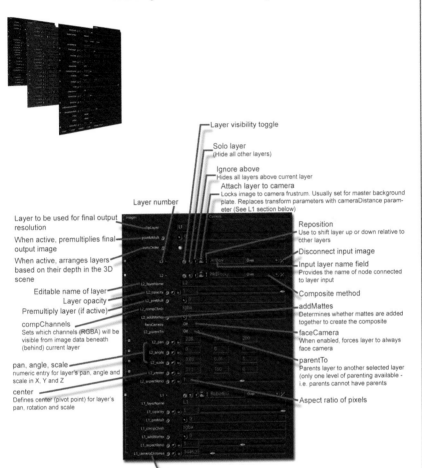

Layer visibility toggle

Solo layer
(Hide all other layers)

Ignore above
Hides all layers above current layer

Attach layer to camera
Locks image to camera frustrum. Usually set for master background plate. Replaces transform parameters with cameraDistance parameter (See L1 section below)

Layer number

Layer to be used for final output resolution

When active, premultiplies final output image

When active, arranges layers based on their depth in the 3D scene

Editable name of layer

Layer opacity

Premultiply layer (if active)

compChannels
Sets which channels (RGBA) will be visible from image data beneath (behind) current layer

pan, angle, scale
numeric entry for layer's pan, angle and scale in X, Y and Z

center
Defines center (pivot point) for layer's pan, rotation and scale

Reposition
Use to shift layer up or down relative to other layers

Disconnect input image

Input layer name field
Provides the name of node connected to layer input

Composite method

addMattes
Determines whether mattes are added together to create the composite

faceCamera
When enabled, forces layer to always face camera

parentTo
Parents layer to another selected layer (only one level of parenting available - i.e. parents cannot have parents

Aspect ratio of pixels

cameraDistance
Determines distance of layer to camera. Only available when "Attach layer to camera" has been activated. Layer automatically scales to fit frame as distance is modified.

Interface

Image

Color

Filter

Key

Layer

Transform

Warp

Other

Scripting

Customizing

Keyboard

# MultiPlane

## Anatomy of the MultiPlane Camera Tab

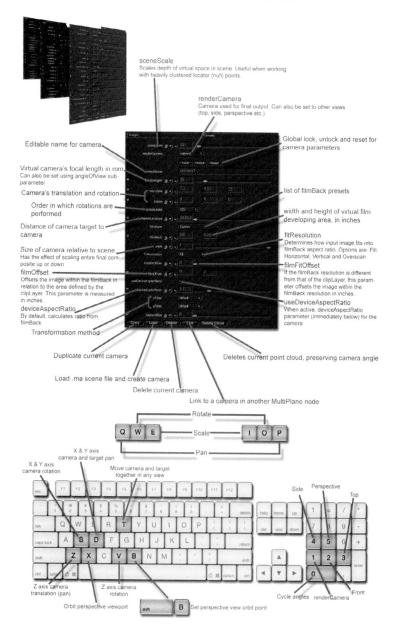

sceneScale
Scales depth of virtual space in scene. Useful when working
with heavily clustered locator (null) points.

renderCamera
Camera used for final output. Can also be set to other views
(top, side, perspective etc.)

Editable name for camera

Global lock, unlock and reset for
camera parameters

Virtual camera's focal length in mm.
Can also be set using angleOfView sub-
parameter

Camera's translation and rotation

list of filmBack presets

Order in which rotations are
performed

width and height of virtual film
developing area, in inches

Distance of camera target to
camera

fitResolution
Determines how input image fits into
filmBack aspect ratio. Options are: Fill,
Horizontal, Vertical and Overscan

Size of camera relative to scene
Has the effect of scaling entire final composite up or down

filmFitOffset
If the filmBack resolution is different
from that of the clipLayer, this parameter offsets the image within the
filmBack resolution in inches.

filmOffset
Offsets the image within the filmBack in
relation to the area defined by the
clipLayer. This parameter is measured
in inches.

useDeviceAspectRatio
When active, deviceAspectRatio
parameter (immediately below) for the
camera

deviceAspectRatio
By default, calculates ratio from
filmBack

Transformation method

Duplicate current camera

Deletes current point cloud, preserving camera angle

Load .ma scene file and create camera

Delete current camera

Link to a camera in another MultiPlane node

Rotate

Q  W  E          Scale          I  O  P

Pan

X & Y axis
camera and target pan

X & Y axis
camera rotation

Move camera and target
together in any view

Side    Perspective

Top

Z axis camera
translation (pan)

Z axis camera
rotation

Cycle angles   renderCamera

Front

Orbit perspective viewport

shift  B  Get perspective view orbit point

The Transform tab contains the tools used to move things around – pan, scale, rotate, perspective shift etc. It also contains the tracking tools and tools for modifying resolution and limiting Shake's Infinite Workspace.

## Basic Transform Operators

| | AutoAlign | Stitches together image sequences to create a single, panoramic image. Also very useful for cleanplating, aligning two similar images to generate the cleanplate. |
|---|---|---|
| | CameraShake | Provides random jitter of the image using continuous noise |
| | CornerPin | Either pins the image into the four corners or else extracts the image from the four corners to make it square when *inverseTransform* is applied. Combined with a **Stabilize** node with *inverseTransform* set to match, makes a very elegant matchmove workflow. |
| | Flip | Inverts (mirrors) the image vertically |
| | Flop | Inverts (mirrors) the image horizontally |
| | Move2D | A combination of **Pan**, **Scale**, **Rotate** and **Shear**. It's the most common transform operator since all transforms can be done in one place; there's no rendering advantage to using the individual nodes. See page 77 for more OSC details. |
| | Move3D | Same controls as **Move2D**, but with the addition of a third axis camera control. *FieldOfView* parameter must be set before any of the Z controls will have an effect. |
| | Orient | Flips, flops and rotates the image in 90 degree increments |
| | Pan | Moves the image horizontally and vertically. Information on page 77 for **Move2D** applies to **Pan** as well. |
| | Rotate | Rotates the image. Information on page 77 for **Move2D** applies to **Rotate** as well. |
| | Scale | Scales the image larger or smaller without changing the width and height of the frame (resolution). Information on page 77 for **Move2D** applies to **Scale** as well. |

## The Transform Operators

| | Scroll | Same as *Pan*, but image wraps around whenever it goes off the screen. (Compare to Offset in Photoshop) |
|---|---|---|
| | SetDOD | Sets the Domain of Definition (the pixels in an image frame that Shake will perform future operations on) for an image without changing image width and height (resolution). |
| | Shear | Shears the image up and down, or left and right. |

## Anatomy of AutoAlign

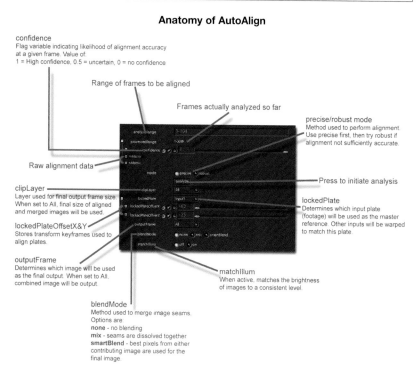

confidence
Flag variable indicating likelihood of alignment accuracy at a given frame. Value of:
1 = High confidence, 0.5 = uncertain, 0 = no confidence

Range of frames to be aligned

Frames actually analyzed so far

precise/robust mode
Method used to perform alignment. Use precise first, then try robust if alignment not sufficiently accurate.

Raw alignment data

Press to initiate analysis

clipLayer
Layer used for final output frame size. When set to All, final size of aligned and merged images will be used.

lockedPlate
Determines which input plate (footage) will be used as the master reference. Other inputs will be warped to match this plate.

lockedPlateOffsetX&Y
Stores transform keyframes used to align plates.

outputFrame
Determines which image will be used as the final output. When set to All, combined image will be output.

matchIllum
When active, matches the brightness of images to a consistent level.

blendMode
Method used to merge image seams.
Options are:
none - no blending
mix - seams are dissolved together
smartBlend - best pixels from either contributing image are used for the final image.

## Anatomy of Move2D's On Screen Controls (OSC)

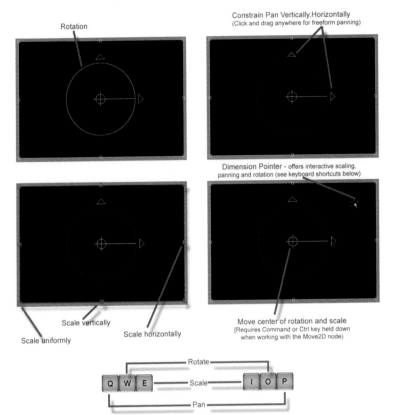

Rotation

Constrain Pan Vertically,Horizontally
(Click and drag anywhere for freeform panning)

Dimension Pointer - offers interactive scaling,
panning and rotation (see keyboard shortcuts below)

Scale vertically

Scale uniformly

Scale horizontally

Move center of rotation and scale
(Requires Command or Ctrl key held down
when working with the Move2D node)

Rotate
Q  W  E  ——— Scale ——— I  O  P
Pan

## The Transform Operators

Shake contains three tracking nodes. The tracking engine is identical in each, it's the way they apply the data that differentiates them.

| | | |
|---|---|---|
| Tracker | **Tracker** | Just the raw tracker. It's purely a tracking engine and a data container. Its usefulness is in having other nodes link to that data. It can also have an unlimited number of tracking points. |
| Stabilize | **Stabilize** | The most versatile of the tracking nodes, it tracks points in an image then applies a pan, rotation, scale or perspective shift in the opposite direction to stabilize the footage. Despite its name, setting the *inverseTransform* parameter to "match" causes it to operate as a match-move. For matchmoving, first track the background footage, then remove the node and attach it to the foreground, setting the *inverseTransform* to "match". |
| MatchMove | **MatchMove** | Tracks points in the image on the background input, then applies a matchmove to the image on the foreground input. Includes a layer operation to composite the two images together. Defaults to displaying background only. Image to be tracked must be attached to the background (second) input. Includes a corner pinning utility, but a more elegant solution is to use a **CornerPin** and **Stabilize** node together, taking advantage of their concatenation. **Note:** despite the lack of a "C" in the icon, **MatchMove** *will* concatenate with transform operators coming into the foreground input (but not transform operators placed after the node). |
| SmoothCam | **SmoothCam** | Automatically smooths or stabilizes motion in an image sequence. A "one-click" solution, **SmoothCam** automatically identifies trackable regions in the image. |

### Tracker On Screen Controls (OSC)

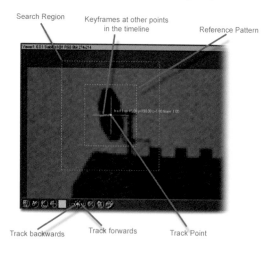

Search Region

Keyframes at other points in the timeline

Reference Pattern

Track backwards    Track forwards    Track Point

## Anatomy of a Tracker Node

**Reference Tolerance**
The point at which the *referenceBehavior* will kick in. When the correlation value (Shake's calculation of its likelihood of having correctly detected the target) for a track drops to this value, then *referenceBehavior* will be initiated.

**Sub-pixel Resolution**
The fractions of a pixel the tracker will search for the new location of the tracking target. For values other than the radio button presets and type a custom fraction into the entry field to the right.

**matchSpace**
Determines which color attributes will be used for the track - luminance (most common), saturation or hue.

Frame range to be tracked

**Reference Behavior**
**use start frame**
Continue using the reference snapshot from the frame at which the track was started
**update every frame**
Regardless of the correlation and reference tolerance, always use the previous frame's identified tracking target as the new reference snapshot.
**update from keyframes**
update reference snapshot from last frame that had a valid keyframe
**update if above reference tolerance**
Continue to update as long as correlation is above reference tolerance
**update if below reference tolerance**
If correlation drops below reference tolerance, then update snapshot from the last good frame. Very useful for gradual perspective shifts in the tracking target

**Reference Tolerance**
The point at which the *referenceBehavior* will kick in. When the correlation value (Shake's calculation of its likelihood of having correctly detected the target) for a track drops to this value, then *referenceBehavior* will be initiated.

**Reference Behavior**
**stop**
The track has evidently gone horribly wrong, so cease tracking.
**predict location and create key**
Predict the new position based on the vector of the last two track points
**predict location and don't create key**
As above, but refrains from placing a key. Very useful for when target passes temporarily behind an object.
**don't predict location**
Continue to look in the same location, but don't create any keyframes
**use existing key to predict location**
Allows user to intelligently create "helper" points when an object is obscured by an object or extreme motion blur.

**matchSpace**
Determines the weight given to the three color channels in contributing to the tracked image. It's very good practice to examine the red, green and blue channels prior to tracking to determine which contains the sharpest, highest contrast.

**track[x]Name Section**
The area where tracking data is stored. *track[x]X, track[x]Y* and *track[x]Correlation* store keyframes for every tracked frame. There's one section for every tracked point. When linking to the parameters, the section header is unnecessary; only the parameter name is required (eg. Tracker1.track1X, not Tracker1.track1Name.track1X).

**Pre-process and Blur Amount**
Activate to apply a slight blur prior to tracking when extreme grain variation will mislead the tracker. *blurAmount* determines the intensity of the blur.

# The Transform Operators

## Anatomy of SmoothCam

Source image input

Mask image input
Mask used to isolate features to track.
White areas of the mask **will not** be tracked
Black areas of the mask **will** be tracked.

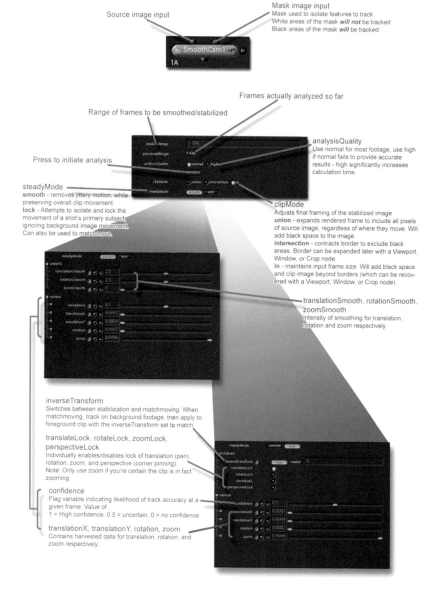

Frames actually analyzed so far

Range of frames to be smoothed/stabilized

analysisQuality
Use normal for most footage, use high
if normal fails to provide accurate
results - high significantly increases
calculation time.

Press to initiate analysis

steadyMode
**smooth** - removes jittery motion, while
preserving overall clip movement
**lock** - Attempts to isolate and lock the
movement of a shot's primary subject,
ignoring background image movement.
Can also be used to matchmove.

clipMode
Adjusts final framing of the stabilized image
**union** - expands rendered frame to include all pixels
of source image, regardless of where they move. Will
add black space to the image.
**intersection** - contracts border to exclude black
areas. Border can be expanded later with a Viewport,
Window, or Crop node.
**in** - maintains input frame size. Will add black space
and clip image beyond borders (which can be recov-
ered with a Viewport, Window, or Crop node).

translationSmooth, rotationSmooth,
zoomSmooth
Intensity of smoothing for translation,
rotation and zoom respectively.

inverseTransform
Switches between stabilization and matchmoving. When
matchmoving, track on background footage, then apply to
foreground clip with the inverseTransform set to match.

translateLock, rotateLock, zoomLock,
perspectiveLock
Individually enables/disables lock of translation (pan),
rotation, zoom, and perspective (corner pinning).
Note: Only use zoom if you're certain the clip is in fact
zooming.

confidence
Flag variable indicating likelihood of track accuracy at a
given frame. Value of
1 = High confidence, 0.5 = uncertain, 0 = no confidence

translationX, translationY, rotation, zoom
Contains harvested data for translation, rotation, and
zoom respectively.

## Resolution Modifiers

| | | |
|---|---|---|
| Crop | **Crop** | Cuts off the borders of the image<br>**Sets DOD to the borders of the image (eliminates image data outside borders).** |
| Fit | **Fit** | Resizes the image down, but maintains the aspect ratio of the image by padding one axis with black |
| Resize | **Resize** | Scales the image resolution, possibly changing the aspect ratio. Entry is via width and height, making it a perfect way to quickly change format resolutions. E.g. square 720x540 (or 768x576 – we love you PAL) to D1 720x486 (or 720x576). |
| Viewport | **Viewport** | Identical to **Crop**, but *doesn't* set DOD (image data beyond the border is preserved and can be revealed to screen again by a future operation) |
| Window | **Window** | Similar to **Crop**, except you supply a lower-left corner and output resolution. **Sets DOD to the borders of the image (eliminates image data outside borders).** |
| Zoom | **Zoom** | Similar to **Resize**, except you supply the scaling factors. |

The Warp tab contains operators that displace pixels by varying amounts causing distortions in the image – rippling, bubbling, smearing, "melting", heat haze, glass refractions etc.

| | DisplaceX, WarpX | **DisplaceX** displaces the pixels in one image according to the values of pixels in a second image. The relationship is set up via user-defined expressions. Useful for UV texture mapping inside of Shake when used with UV render passes. **Note:** if you're experiencing unexpected results, most often it's because the *xDelta* and *yDelta* are set too low. These must be set to the maximum distance a pixel will be displaced. **WarpX** also generates distortion based on user-defined expressions, but without a 2$^{nd}$ control image. |
|---|---|---|
| | IDisplace | Similar to **DisplaceX**, but without the user-defined expressions. The horizontal and vertical displacement can independently be set to use the red, green, blue or alpha channel of the second image. For a given pixel in the first image, if the chosen matte channel (from the second image) has a black pixel, there will be no displacement of the pixel. If it has a white pixel, it will move the number of pixels designated by *xScale* (or *yScale* in the case of the vertical channel). If it has some value in between, the pixel will move by that fraction of *xScale*. Very useful for simulating refraction, shadow displacement over uneven surfaces etc.<br><br>To get the idea, attach some footage to the first input and a **Checker** to the second, and then adjust the *xScale*. After that, attach an **RGrad**. That should clear it all up. |
| | LensWarp | Used to eliminate or introduce lens distortion for an image. Simply draw open splines along features in the image that were naturally straight on set, then press the analyze button to calculate the lens distortion. To introduce a matching distortion, extract the node, apply it to another undistorted node, and set to Distort. |
| | Morpher | An extension of the **Warper**, the Morpher node warps features in Image A to match the shape of corresponding features in Image B. It also warps features in Image B to match the shape of corresponding features in Image A. These warps occur over time so that as Image A warps into B, image B is moving from a fully warped state to its original unwarped shape. A cross-dissolve occurring at the same time from Image A to Image B completes the illusion of Image A "becoming" Image B. |

| | PinCushion | Generates a concave or convex distortion around the centre of the image, with independent control of horizontal and vertical distortion. If the lens focal point is off axis (not centered), sandwich the PinCushion between two **Move2Ds** - copy the first **Move2D**, then CTRL-SHIFT-V paste to create a linked version, activating the *inverseTransform* on the second **Move2D**. Pan the first **Move2D** to center on the focal point. Make sure the *xPan* and *yPan* are rounded to the nearest integer (i.e. no decimal places) to prevent sub-pixel softening. |
|---|---|---|
| | Randomize | Takes your pixels and shakes them all around. The amplitude parameters determine how far a pixel is allowed to travel from its home. |
| | Turbulate | Jitters the pixels around with continuous noise, creating wavy effects. Good for heat exhaust effects. Extremely render intensive |
| | Twirl | A rotational warp |
| | Warper | Uses spline curves and shapes to define localized warping of the image. Pixels under or near a source shape will displace towards the destination shape. Additional boundary shapes are used to keep specified areas of the image from being displaced. |
| | WarpX | See *DisplaceX* above. |

# The Warp Tools

## Anatomy of the Morpher/Warper Viewer Controls

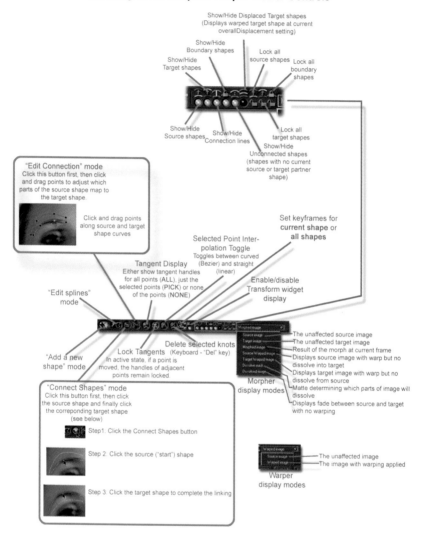

Can't find it anywhere else? Chances are it's in the *Other* tab. It contains miscellaneous utility nodes, including the measurement tools **PlotScanline**, **Histogram** and **PixelAnalyzer**. This is also the location of the very important **Bytes** operator, used for promoting and demoting the bit-depth of images.

| | | |
|---|---|---|
| AddBorders | **AddBorders** | Evenly adds black letterboxing to the horizontal or vertical, useful for widescreen display in 4:3 aspect etc. Negative values will crop the image but preserve the infinite workspace (and DOD). |
| AddShadow | **AddShadow** | A macro, it takes the image and places a "shadow" behind it according to the alpha channel. Use on premultiplied images. You can control the shadow softness, opacity, position and color. To scale or otherwise modify the shadow, use in conjunction with a **Move2D**. |
| Bytes | **Bytes** | Promotes or demotes the bit depth of an image between 1 (8 bit), 2 (16 bit) or 4 (32 bit – float) bytes. **Note:** Shake has no 10 bit mode; 10 bit images are automatically promoted to 16 bit on FileIn. |
| Cache | **Cache** | Allows you to cache designated sections of your script either to disk or into system RAM. Very useful when a major section of your script is completed; simply cache the output of that section to keep Shake from re-evaluating it during future composites. |
| DeInterlace | **DeInterlace** | Interpolates 2 video fields to generate a deinterlaced frame. **Note:** should not be used for general video work; the **FileIn** handles correct deinterlacing workflow in Shake. Should only be used in situations where a still video frame needs to be held over time. |
| DropShadow | **DropShadow** | A macro, it sets the color of the visible channels to a user-defined color and provides opacity and softness controls |
| Field | **Field** | Extracts a half-height image based on one video field |
| Histogram | **Histogram** | Plots a histogram of the input image. Also available as a viewer script. For an often more useful luminance histogram, apply a **Monochrome** node to the input. |
| PixelAnalyzer | **PixelAnalyzer** | Tracks a user-defined region of the image and records the average, minimum and maximum values for the RGBA channels. The recorded values can then be linked to from other nodes. Useful for matching foreground composite elements to lighting flicker in background plate. |

| | | |
|---|---|---|
| PlotScanline | **PlotScanline** | Generates a plot of pixel values across a one-pixel high horizontal slice of the image (determined by the *line* parameter). The brighter a pixel's value, the higher it will appear on the plot. If data is too scattered to detect trends, try applying a *Blur* before the PlotScanline to smooth out the information. Also available as a viewer script. |
| Select | **Select** | Allows you to connect an unlimited number of inputs and choose which to pass through to the output via an integer flag (or the GUI slider). Very useful for creating radio button options in macros, or for creating quick cuts between different pieces of footage. |
| SwapFields | **SwapFields** | Reverses the field dominance. |
| Tile | **Tile** | Makes smaller, tiled versions of the image. Useful when used with seamless textures. |
| TimeX | **TimeX** | Used to alter the timing of an image via user-defined mathematical expressions. You can only have **one** TimeX node per *FileIn*. Images can also be retimed and ramped in the *FileIn* node. |
| TLCalibrate | **TLCalibrate** | A node used to calibrate your Viewer in order to apply a color correction to simulate the look of output devices such as HD monitors and film projectors. Use in conjunction with the *Truelight VLUT* or *Truelight* node in the Color tab. |
| Transition | **Transition** | Used to create basic cut, dissolve and wipe transitions between 2 footage elements. Wipes can be useful for compares and quick cleanplating. |

## Links and Expressions

You can modify any parameter with an expression by typing in the text field. Expressions can be mathematical functions, conditional statements, or link one parameter to another.

## Creating and Removing Local Variables

You can create additional parameters of your own, with extra sliders and text entry fields, in order to build more complex expressions with interactive input.

**To create a local variable within a node in your script:**

1. Pick the node you want to add a local variable to, and open its parameters into the Parameters tab.
2. Right-click anywhere within the Parameters tab (not directly on a field), then choose *Create Local Variable* from the shortcut menu.
3. When the *Local Variable Parameters* window appears, define the settings that variable will be created with.

- *Variable name*: The name for that variable that appears in the Parameters tab.
- *Variable type:* Whether the variable is a float (decimal places of precision), a string (alpha-numeric text), or an integer (whole numbers).
- *Slider Low Val*: For float and int variables, the lowest value the slider will represent.
- *Slider Hi Val*: For float and int variables, the highest value the slider will represent.

4. When you're done, click *OK* to create the variable and go back to your project, *cancel* to close the window without creating a new variable, or *next* to continue creating new variables.

Interface

Image

Color

Filter

Key

Layer

Transform

Warp

Expressions    Other

Macros    Scripting

The Terminal    Customizing

Keyboard

New local variables that you create appear within a subtree at the bottom of the other node parameters. This subtree appears only after at least one new variable has been created, and is named localParameters.

Once created, your own local variables can be used and referenced by expressions just like any other parameter in Shake.

**To remove a local variable:**
1. Right-click anywhere within the Parameters tab (not directly on a field), then choose *Delete Local Variable* from the shortcut menu.
2. When the Delete Local Variable window appears, choose a local variable to delete from the pop-up menu, then click *OK*.

For a detailed tutorial on using local variables in expressions, see Tutorial 4, "Working With Expressions," in the Shake 4 *Tutorials*.

## Expressions

The following section provides examples of useful expressions that can help out by doing your work for you. In any parameter, you can combine any value with a math expression, trigonometry function, an animated curve, a variable, or even a conditional expression.

For example, as mentioned above, the center of an image can be found by using:

xCenter = width/2
yCenter = height/2

These equations take the per-image width and height variables and divide them by 2.

You can type an expression in any field. Some nodes, such as *ColorX*, *WarpX*, and *TimeX*, even support locally declared variables. For more information and a list of examples, see "*ColorX*" on page 647 of the Shake documentation.

If you are using the command-line method, you may need to enclose your expressions in quotes to avoid problems with the operating system reading the command. For example, don't use:

```
shake my_image.iff -rot 45*6
```

Instead, use:

```
shake my_image.iff -rot "45*6"
```

### Some Useful Expressions

| | |
|---|---|
| `1/2.2` | 1 divided by 2.2. Gives you the inverse of 2.2 gamma. |
| `2*Linear(0,0@1,200@20)` | Multiplies the value of an animated curve by 2. |
| `2*my_curve` | Multiplies a variable by 2. |
| `sqrt(my_curve-my_center)/2` | Subtracts *my_center* from *my_curve*, takes the result square root, and then divides by 2. |
| `time>20?1:0` | If time is greater than 20, then the parameter is 1, otherwise it equals 0. |
| `cos(time/s)*50` | Gives a smooth ping-pong between -50 and 50. |

### Precedence

The above operators are listed in order of precedence—the order Shake evaluates each operator, left to right. If this is difficult to keep up with (and it is), make liberal use of parentheses to force the order of evaluation. For instance:

```
a = 1 + 2 * 4 -2
```

This expression does "2*4" first, since the "*" has precedence over "+" and "-" which gives you "a=1+8-2." Then from left to right, Shake does "1+8," giving "a=9-2," finally resulting in "a=7." To add and subtract before multiplying, use parentheses to control the evaluation.

```
a = (1 + 2) * (4 - 2)
```

This results in "a=3*2" or "a=6."

**Note:** In any expression, parentheses have the highest precedence.

### Linking Guidelines

To link to another parameter in the same node or in the Globals tab:

You can *Shift+Drag* one parameter name to another, or type in the parameter you want to link to. A sub-text field appears after you type a value and press *Enter*. This image shows a link from yScale to xScale.

*To link to a parameter in a different node:*

Enter the name of the target node, a period, and then the parameter name.

*To clone an entire node:*

Copy and paste the node with *Ctrl+Shift+V*. You then modify the original. Modifying the copy breaks the link on that parameter. To see the links, press *Ctrl+E* in the Node View.

*To create an extra parameter:*

Press the right mouse button in the Parameters tab and select Create Local Variable. You can also do this in the Globals tab.

*To link to a parameter at a different frame:*

Use `parameter@@time` and specify your time. The following example links to the previous frame:

```
Blur1.xPixels@@time-1
```

All of the math functions available in Shake can be found in the *include/nreal.h* file. You can declare your own functions in your own .h file.

To set an expression on a string (text) parameter, you need to add a : (colon) at the start of the expression; otherwise, it is treated as text rather than compiled and evaluated.

### Arithmetic Operators

| | |
|---|---|
| * | Multiply |
| / | Divide |
| + | Add |
| - | Subtract |

### Relational Operators

| | |
|---|---|
| < | Less than |
| > | Greater than |
| <= | Less than or equal to |
| >= | Greater than or equal to |
| == | Equal to |
| != | Not equal to |

### Logical Operators

| | |
|---|---|
| && | And |
| \|\| | Or |
| ! | Not |

### Conditional Expression

expr1?expr2:expr3    If expr1 is true (non-zero), then to expr2, else do expr3.

### Global Variables

time    Current frame number.

# Reference Tables for Functions, Variables, and Expressions

## Image Variables

The following table shows variables that are carried by each node.

| parameterName | Value of *parameterName* from inside of that node. |
|---|---|
| nodeName.parameterName | Value of *parameterName* in nodeName from outside of that node. |
| parameterName@@time | Allows you to access a value at a different frame. For example: *Blur1.xPixel@@(time-3)* looks at the value from 3 frames earlier. |
| bytes | The number of bytes in that image. This takes the input bit depth when called from inside of the node, and the output bit depth when called from outside of the node. |
| width | Width of the image. Takes the input width when called from inside of the node, and the output width when called from outside of the node. |
| height | Height of the image. Takes the input height when called from inside of the node, and the output height when called from outside of the node. |
| _curImageName | Returns the name of the actual file being used for the current frame. Useful when plugged into a Text node: {*FileIn1._curImageName*} |
| dod[0], dod[1], dod[2],dod[3] | The variable for the Domain of Definition (DOD): xMin, yMin, xMax, yMax, respectively. |

The following table shows channel variables used in nodes such as ColorX, LayerX, Reorder, etc. Check the Shake User Manual for specific support of any variable.

## In-Node Variables

| nr, ng, nb, na, nz | New red, green, blue, alpha, Z channel. |
|---|---|
| r, g, b, a, z | Original red, green, blue, alpha, Z channel. |
| l | Luminance channel for Reorder. |
| n | Null channel. Strips out the alpha in Reorder when used like this: rgbn |
| r2, g2, b2, a2, z2 | Second image's channel for LayerX |

**Math Functions**

| | |
|---|---|
| abs(x) | Integer absolute value. abs(-4) = 4. Be careful, as this returns an integer, not a float. Use *fabs* for float. |
| biasedGain(value, gain, bias) | Gives a *ContrastLum*-like curve that gives roll-off between two values. |
| cbrt(x) | Cubic root. cbrt(8) = 2 |
| ceil(x) | Truncates to next integer. ceil(5.3) = 6 |
| clamp(x, lo, hi) | Clamps x to between lo and hi. clamp(1.5,0,1) = 1 |
| exp(x) | Natural exponent. exp(0) = 1 |
| fabs(x) | Float absolute value. fabs(-4.1) = 4.1 |
| floor(x) | Truncates to next lowest integer. floor(5.8) = 5 |
| fmod(x,y) | Float modulus. Returns the remainder in float. fmod(11.45,3) = 2, for example, (3x3+2.45 = 11.45) |
| log(x) | Natural log. log(1) = 0 |
| log10(x) | Returns base 10 log. log10(10) = 1 |
| M_PI | A variable set to pi at 20 decimal places. |
| max(a,b) | Returns maximum between a and b. max(5,10) = 10 |
| max3(a,b,c) | Returns maximum between a, b, and c. max3(5,2,4) = 5 |
| min(a,b) | Returns minimum between a and b. min(5,10) = 5 |
| min3(a,b,c) | Returns minimum between a, b, and c. min3(5,2,4) = 2 |
| a%b | Modulus. 27%20 = 7 |
| pow(x,y) | Returns x to the y power. pow(2,4) = 16 |
| round(x) | Rounds number off. Values below x.5 are rounded to x, values equal to or above x.5 are rounded to x+1. round(4.3) = 4 |
| sqrt(x) | Square root. sqrt(9) = 3 |

## Noise Functions

**Note:** These are ideal for *WarpX* and *ColorX*.

| | |
|---|---|
| noise(seed) | 1-dimensional cubic spline interpolation of noise. |
| noise2d(seed,seed) | 2d noise. |
| noise3d(seed,seed,seed) | 3d noise. |
| noise4d(seed,seed,seed,seed) | 4d noise. |
| lnoise(seed) | 1d linear interpolation of noise. |
| lnoise2d(seed,seed) | 2d noise. |
| lnoise3d(seed,seed,seed) | 3d noise. |
| lnoise4d(seed,seed,seed,seed) | 4d noise. |
| fnoise(x,xScale)<br>fnoise2d(x,y,xScale,yScale)<br>fnoise3d(x, y, z, xScale, yScale, zScale) | 1d fractal noise based on noise(). |
| turbulence(x, xScale)<br>turbulence2d(x, y, xScale, yScale)<br>turbulence3d(x, y, z, xScale, yScale, zScale) | A cheaper, rougher version of fnoise(). Continuous 2d noise. Continuous 3d noise. |
| rnd(seed) | Hash-based pseudo-random numbers. Non-hash based RNG (like rand() or drand48()) should not be used in Shake because they cannot be reproduced from one machine to another. Also, even on the same machine, repeated evaluations of the same node at the same time would produce different results. |
| rnd1d(seed, seed) | 1d random value. |
| rnd2d(seed,seed,seed) | 2d random value. |
| rnd3d(seed,seed,seed,seed) | 3d random value. |
| rnd4d(seed,seed,seed,seed,seed) | 4d random value. |

## Trig Functions (in radians)

| M_PI | A variable set to pi at 20 decimal places. |
|------|--------------------------------------------|
| acos(A) | Arc cosine in radians. |
| asin(A) | Arc sine. |
| atan(A) | Arc tangent. |
| atan2(y,x) | Returns the radian verifying sin(a) = y and cos(a) = x. |
| cos(A) | Cosine. |
| sin(A) | Sin. |

Interface

Image

Color

Filter

Key

Layer

Transform

Warp

Extensions    Other

Macros    Scripting

The Terminal    Customizing    Keyboard

# Reference Tables for Functions, Variables, and Expressions

## Trig Functions (in degrees)

Welcome back to trigonometry! For those who may have forgotten, here is a helpful chart for some commonly used equations.

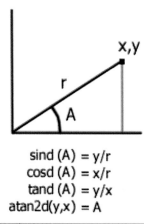

$$\text{sind}\ (A) = y/r$$
$$\text{cosd}\ (A) = x/r$$
$$\text{tand}\ (A) = y/x$$
$$\text{atan2d}(y,x) = A$$

| | |
|---|---|
| acosd(A) | Arc cosine in degrees. |
| asind(A) | Arc sine in degrees. |
| atand(A) | Arc tangent in degrees. |
| atan2d(y,x) | Returns the angle verifying sin(a) = y and cos(a) = x. |
| cosd(A) | Cosine in degrees. |
| distance(x1,y1,x2,y2) | Calculates the distance between two points, (x1,y1) and (x2, y2). |
| sind(A) | Sin in degrees. |
| tand(A) | Tangent in degrees. |

## String Functions

String functions are too complex a topic to do justice to in a quick-reference guide. We'll limit ourselves here to an example. This example takes the *scriptName* parameter and uses the system function echo to print it:

```
extern "C" int system(const char*); const char *z=
stringf("echo%s",scriptName); system(z);
```

To learn more, there are also several examples in Chapter 30, *Installing and Creating Macros*, on page 905 of the Shake User Manual.

## Curve Functions

It's worth noting that the curve functions with implicit time (Linear, CSpline, and so on) all assume that time is the first argument, so the following statements are identical:

```
LinearV(time,0,1@1,20@20)
Linear(0,1@1,20@20)
```

You can, however, adjust the time value explicitly with the V version of each curve type. These are the cycle type codes:
- 0 = KeepValue
- 1 = KeepSlope
- 2 = RepeatValue
- 3 = MirrorValue
- 4 = OffsetValue

| | |
|---|---|
| biasedGain(x,gain,bias) | Gives a smoothly-ramped interpolation between 0 and 1, similar to Shake's contrast curve. *Gain* increases the contrast, and *bias* offsetsthe center. |
| Linear(cycle, value@key1, value@key2,...) | Linear interpolation from value at keyframe 1 to value at keyframe 2, and so on. |
| LinearV(time_value, cycle, value@key1, value@key2,...) | Linear interpolation from value at keyframe 1 to value at keyframe 2, and so on. |
| CSpline(cycle, value@key1, value@key2,...) | Cardinal-spline interpolation, also known as Catmull-Rom splines. |
| CSplineV(time_value, cycle, value@key1, value@key2,...) | Cardinal-spline interpolation, also known as Catmull-Rom splines. |
| JSpline(cycle, value@key1, value@key2,...) | Jeffress-spline interpolation. |
| JSplineV(time_value, cycle, value@key1, value@key2,...) | Jeffress-spline interpolation. |

Interface  Image  Color  Filter  Key  Layer  Transform  Warp  Other  Scripting  Customizing
Expressions  Macros  The Terminal  Keyboard

| | |
|---|---|
| NSpline(cycle, value@key1, value@key2,...) | Natural-spline interpolation. |
| NSplineV(time_value, cycle, value@key1, value@key2,...) | Natural-spline interpolation. |
| Hermite(cycle, [value,tangent1,tangent2]@key1, [value,tangent1,tangent2]@key2,...) | Hermite-spline interpolation. |
| HermiteV(time_value, cycle, [value,tangent1,tangent2]@key1, [value,tangent1,tangent2]@key2,...) | Hermite-spline interpolation. |

## Curve Analysis

The following expressions provide functions for curve analysis.

| | |
|---|---|
| getCurveMinMax(int minOrMax, int begFrame, int endFrame, float curveCurrentValue, const char *curveName); | Float. Returns the min or max value of the specified curve (plug) over the spec ified frame range. If minOrMax is set to 0, then it returns the min value. If minOrMax is set to 1, then it returns the max value. |
| getCurveAvg(int begFrame, int endFrame, float curveCurrentValue, const char *curveName); | Float. Returns the average value of the specified curve over the specified frame range. |

## Using Signal Generators Within Expressions

This section illustrates the use of the various signal generators that are available for Shake expressions. Signal generators can be used to create either predictable or random patterns of values, and mathematically customized to adjust their offset, frequency, and amplitude.

## Signal Generators

The following noise and trig functions all generate changing values over time. To animate a parameter using these functions, you supply the variable time for the function to operate upon.

**Note:** You can copy and paste most of the expressions found in this section into your own scripts for easy use.

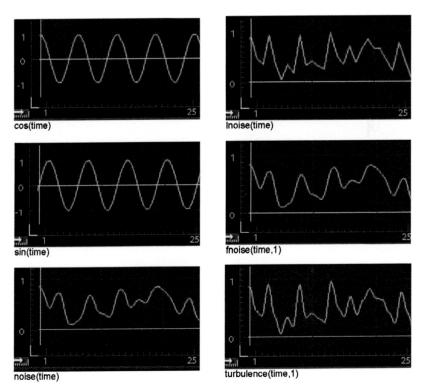

cos(time)

lnoise(time)

sin(time)

fnoise(time,1)

noise(time)

turbulence(time,1)

# Using Signal Generators Within Expressions

**Note:** fnoise() and turbulence() have additional frequency factors to the noise:

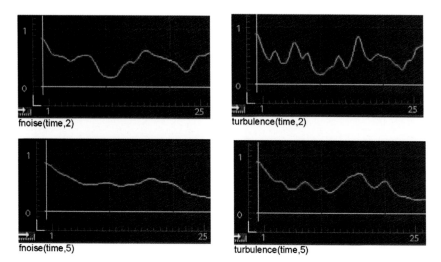

fnoise(time,2)

turbulence(time,2)

fnoise(time,5)

turbulence(time,5)

## Offsetting a Generator Function

To offset a function's starting value, add a value to time.

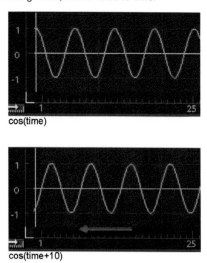

cos(time)

cos(time+10)

## Changing the Frequency of a Generator Function

To change a function's frequency, *multiply* or *divide* time by a value.The exceptions are the noise functions *fnoise()* and *turbulence()*—both of which have frequency controls of their own (values are not modified below 1, so you may still have to modify *time*).

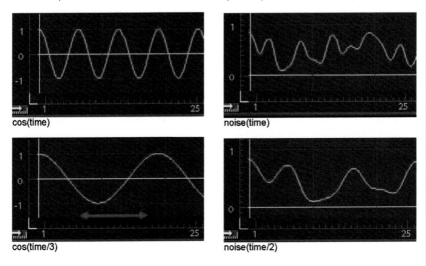

cos(time)

noise(time)

cos(time/3)

noise(time/2)

For more information on noise generators, setting ranges for expressions, and modifying noise, see *Expressions and Scripting* in the Shake User Manual.

## The nglrender Node

nGL is a software-based emulation of OpenGL. It contains only a subset of the OpenGL command set (for example, there is no texture mapping support). It can be used from within Macros to create custom shapes.

The ngl functions have similar programming constructs to OpenGL:

```
nglPushMatrix() ... nglPopMatrix()
nglBegin(NGL_PRIMITIVE) ... nglEnd()
```

### nGL Functions

### Geometry Primitives

NGL_POINTS
NGL_LINES
NGL_LINE_STRIP
NGL_LINE_LOOP
NGL_TRIANGLES
NGL_TRIANGLE_STRIP
NGL_TRIANGLE_FAN
NGL_QUADS
NGL_QUAD_STRIP
NGL_POLYGON
NGL_BEZIER - used by QuickShape and RotoShape

### Color Control and Point/Vertex Drawing

void nglColor3f(float, float, float);
void nglColor4f(float, float, float, float);
void nglPoint2f(float, float);
void nglPointSize(float);
void nglVertex2f(float, float);
void nglVertex2v(const float *);
void nglVertex3f(float, float, float);
void nglVertex3v(const float *);

### Program Control and Transformations

void nglBegin(int);
void nglEnd();
void nglFlush();
void nglMatrixMode(int);
void nglPushMatrix();
void nglPopMatrix();
void nglPerspective(float, float, float, float, float, float);
void nglRotatef(float, float, float, float);
void nglScalef(float, float, float);
void nglTranslatef(float, float, float);

## Font Control and String Drawing

```
void nglFont(const char *, float, float);
void nglFontAlignment(int);
void nglFontLeading(float);
void nglFontKerning(float);
void nglFontQuality(float);
void nglString(const char *);
void nglCMove2f(float, float);
const char * nglFontList();
```

**An nglrender sample**

```
//The Arrow ngl Macro
//Peter Warner
//Nov 1, 2001

image Arrow(
        image Input=0,
        int width = GetDefaultWidth(),
        int height = GetDefaultHeight(),
        float red=1,
        float green=0,
        float blue=0,
        float arrowWidth=8,
        float headLength=arrowWidth*2,
        float headWidth=arrowWidth*2.5,
        int tailArrow = 0,
        float shadowOpacity=.75,
        float shadowFuzziness=16,
        float xOffset=5,
        float yOffset=-5,
        float pos1X = 20,
        float pos1Y = 20,
        float pos2X = 100,
        float pos2Y = 100
)
{
        arrows = NGLRender(
        width, height, 1,
        "
// initial calculations
        curve float a= atan2d(pos1Y-pos2Y, pos1X-pos2X);
        curve float dist = distance(pos2X,pos2Y, pos1X, pos1Y);
        curve float halfWidth = arrowWidth/2;
```

## The nglrender Node

```
//Position
    nglPushMatrix();
            //nglTranslatef(-pos1X,-pos1Y,0.0f);
            nglRotatef(a,0.0f,0.0f,1.0f);
            nglTranslatef(pos2X,pos2Y,0.0f);

//main poly
        if (tailArrow==0) {
        nglBegin(NGL_POLYGON);
                nglColor4f(red,green,blue,1);
                nglVertex2f(0,-halfWidth);
                nglVertex2f(dist-headLength,-halfWidth);
                nglVertex2f(dist-headLength, -headWidth/2);
                nglVertex2f(dist, 0);
                nglVertex2f(dist-headLength, headWidth/2);
                nglVertex2f(dist-headLength,halfWidth);
                nglVertex2f(0,halfWidth);
        nglEnd();
        } else {
        nglBegin(NGL_POLYGON);
                nglColor4f(red,green,blue,1);
                nglVertex2f(0,0);
                nglVertex2f(headLength,-headWidth/2);
                nglVertex2f(headLength,-halfWidth);
                nglVertex2f(dist-headLength,-halfWidth);
                nglVertex2f(dist-headLength, -headWidth/2);
                nglVertex2f(dist, 0);
                nglVertex2f(dist-headLength, headWidth/2);
                nglVertex2f(dist-headLength,halfWidth);
                nglVertex2f(headLength,halfWidth);
                nglVertex2f(headLength,headWidth/2);
        nglEnd();
        }
    nglPopMatrix();

        "
        );
        Shadow = AddShadow(arrows,xOffset,yOffset,shadowFuzziness,0,0,0,
                shadowOpacity);
        Over1 = Over(Shadow,Input,1);
        return Over1;
}
```

# Anatomy of the MacroMaker

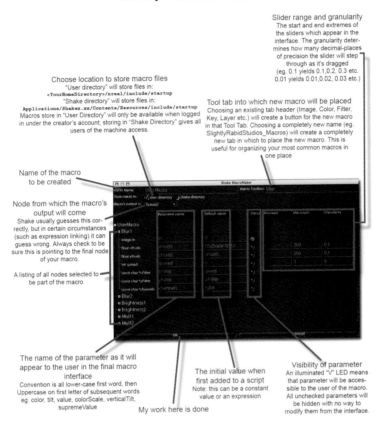

**Slider range and granularity**
The start and end extremes of the sliders which appear in the interface. The granularity determines how many decimal-places of precision the slider will step through as it's dragged (eg. 0.1 yields 0.1,0.2, 0.3 etc. 0.01 yields 0.01,0.02, 0.03 etc.)

**Choose location to store macro files**
"User directory" will store files in:
`<YourHomeDirectory>/nreal/include/startup`
"Shake directory" will store files in:
`Applications/Shake.xx/Contents/Resources/include/startup`
Macros store in "User Directory" will only be available when logged in under the creator's account; storing in "Shake Directory" gives all users of the machine access.

**Tool tab into which new macro will be placed**
Choosing an existing tab header (Image, Color, Filter, Key, Layer etc.) will create a button for the new macro in that Tool Tab. Choosing a completely new name (eg. SlightlyRabidStudios_Macros) will create a completely new tab in which to place the new macro. This is useful for organizing your most common macros in one place

**Name of the macro to be created**

**Node from which the macro's output will come**
Shake usually guesses this correctly, but in certain circumstances (such as expression linking) it can guess wrong. Always check to be sure this is pointing to the final node of your macro.

A listing of all nodes selected to be part of the macro

**The name of the parameter as it will appear to the user in the final macro interface**
Convention is all lower-case first word, then Uppercase on first letter of subsequent words eg. color, tilt, value, colorScale, verticalTilt, supremeValue

**The initial value when first added to a script**
Note: this can be a constant value or an expression

My work here is done

**Visibility of parameter**
An illuminated "V" LED means that parameter will be accessible to the user of the macro. All unchecked parameters will be hidden with no way to modify them from the interface.

# How to Install a Macro

Shake has a healthy community of users who have created many, many free macros for use with Shake (for example, check out www.highend2d.com). The biggest problem most people have is figuring out how to install them. Here's the skinny:

There are three main parts to a macro: the macro script itself, the macro's UI script and the icon image. (Note: if you're only executing Shake processes from the terminal, you only actually need the primary macro script – the other files are for the benefit of the Shake GUI.) More complex macros containing radio buttons etc. also have additional images for these buttons. Let's take a look at how to install a very popular fictitious macro, **academyAwardGenerator**.

# Macros

Downloading the **academyAwardGenerator** macro, we find 3 main files: **academyAwardGenerator.h**, **academyAwardGeneratorUI.h**, and **Other**. AcademyAwardGenerator.nri.

First we need to install the macro script, **academyAwardGenerator.h**. This installs in the following location:

If any of these folders don't exist (and they won't if you've never created or previously installed a macro) just right-click in the Finder window and choose "New Folder". **Note:** Shake is case-sensitive, so make sure you type the folder labels all lower-case.

Next we need to install the **academyAwardGeneratorUI.h** file, the file that tells Shake how to draw the user interface for the macro. This installs in a "ui" folder directly beneath the "folder" in which we just installed the main macro script.

Finally, the icon for the macro's button (which appears in the Tools Tab) needs to be put in its proper place. Our macro "lives" in the *Other* tab, hence the naming convention: **Other. AcademyAwardGenerator.nri**.

Any images to be used for radio buttons should go in the "ux" folder inside the "icons" folder. Usually these are stored in additional subfolders; check any documentation that comes with the macro as to how these should be laid out inside "ux".

Quit Shake and re-launch to discover your new macro. If it doesn't work, you most likely mistyped a folder or file name (or are trying to install a poorly written macro). You can check the Console (found in Applications/Utilities) to try to diagnose the problem.

**Note:** You must exit Shake and re-launch in order to load the new macros into the interface; Shake only looks for the macros when starting up (hence the reason for putting the macros in a folder called "Startup")

## Using the Terminal

Theoretically, you can run all of Shake's functions in the command-line Terminal. For nodes such as RotoShape and ColorCorrect, however, the Terminal is not practical since you do not have the feedback or the controls. The Terminal is perfect for repetitive commands that you already know the parameters you want:

- Resize files
- Format change
- Add or remove channels or bit depth
- Simple standard color corrections (such as gamma)
- Apply custom macros that repeat many commands with one function
- Launch flipbooks or get image information
- Execute saved scripts from the interface

### Converting Files

| Action | Command |
|---|---|
| Set the time range (for example, 1-100, 10-20, 1-20x3 or 1,5,10- 20). | -t <timeRange> |
| Write a file to disk | -fo <name.frame.ext> |
| Frame variable for padded numbers (0001, 0002, 0003). | # |
| Variable for unpadded numbers (1, 2, 3). 3-place padding, etc. | @ @@@ |

### Example: Converting Cineon files to Targa files

The following command converts 100 Cineon files (named *myInFile.0001.cin*, *myInFile.0002.cin*, etc.), to targa files (named *myOutFile.1.tga, myOutFile.2.tga*, etc.):

```
shake myInFile.#.cin -fo myOutFile.@.tga -t 1-100 -v
```

Special formatting is required on the command-line to write QuickTime files:

```
shake myInFile.#.cin -v -fo myQTFile.mov QuickTime <codec> <compression>
<fps>
```

where *codec* is the codec you want to use (if you don't know, put *Default*), and compression goes from 0 to 1.

## Common Tasks

Use the commands on the following page to perform common tasks. Often, it is not necessary to supply every value. For example, for `-contrastlum`, you can supply the contrast without entering the center and rolloff. Additionally, you don't have to type in the entire word (as long as there isn't any ambiguity), so `-by` should work for `-bytes`.

## Examples

Use the following to render a script that has **_FileOut_** commands saved in it. The time command is optional, as it may be in the script:

```
shake -exec myscript.shk -v -t 1-30
```

To convert bit depth, use the `-bytes` command. This turns 100 10-bit Cineon files to 8-bit TIFF files.

```
shake myfile.#.cin -bytes 1 -fo myNewFile.@.tif -t 1-100
```

### Common Execution Commands

| Action | Command |
|---|---|
| Render a script's FileOut commands. | -exec <scriptname> |
| Turn off antialiasing. | -fast |
| Load the second image to compare; use Alt+drag to wipe between the images. | -compare <image> |
| Verbose | -v |
| Very Verbose (Print render times on the fly) | -vv |
| Set proxy scale to full resolution (aspect ratio of 1) | -proxyscale <scale> <aspect> |
| Render the proxies from a script (used with exec and createdirs). | -renderproxies p1 p2 p3 |
| Turn off antialiasing. | -fast |
| Launch the documentation. | -doc |
| List information about the image. | -info |
| List out commands matching the function you supply. | -help <function> |

**Common Functions**

| Action | Command |
|---|---|
| Change bit depth. You can select 1 (8 bits), 2 (16 bits), or 4 (float). | -bytes <bytes> |
| Zoom the image by a factor. If you want to zoom both the x and y by the same amount, use -z. | -z <factor> <br> -zoom <xZoom> <yZoom> |
| Specify the explicit resolution. May alter your aspect ratio. | -resize <xSize> <ySize> |
| Specify the explicit resolution. This maintains your aspect ratio. See also AutoFit in "Cookbook - Transform Macros." | -fit <xSize> <ySize> |
| Crop the image. | -crop <left> <bottom> <right> <top> |
| Remove an alpha channel. | -setalpha 0 |
| Add an alpha channel and set it to solid white. | -setalpha 1 |
| Turn a 3-channel RGB image to a 1- channel image. | -forcergb |
| Lower or raise the saturation. A value of 1 means no change. | -saturation <value> |
| Add or subtract color. 0 means no change. You can supply up to 5 values. | -add <red> <green> <blue> <alpha> <depth> |
| Multiply the RGB channels uniformly. | -bright <value> |
| Fade the image. | -fade <value> |
| Multiply individual channels. | -mult <red> <green> <blue> <alpha> <depth> |
| Gamma function. | -gamma <red> <green> <blue> <alpha> |
| Contrast function. | -contrastlum <contrast> <center> <rolloff> |
| Composite an image over something. | -over <backgroundImage> |
| Composite an image under something. | -under <foregroundImage> |

You can customize Shake through the creation and editing of files in specific directories. You can control many UI features, memory and cache usage, as well as create your own functions.

## Location of Customization Files

Setup files can go in one of three places. The startup directory also has a ui subdirectory.
- <ShakeDir>/Contents/Plugins/startup (<ShakeDir>/include/startup on non- OSX)
- $HOME/nreal/include/startup/
- $NR_INCLUDE_PATH/startup/

The important *nreal.h* and *nrui.h* files, that can also be used as references for how to create things, are stored under *<ShakeDir>/Contents/Resources* (*<ShakeDir>/include/* on non-OSX). All files in these directories must have a .h extension to be read; to disable a file, remove the .h extension. Macros and machine-based settings go in *startup*. UI settings and Macro UI files go into the *ui* directory. The chart shows into which directory to place the following settings:

## Memory/Cache Management Settings

| Action | Folder | Code |
|---|---|---|
| Set memory available for script nodes. This can typically remain under 96 MB. | startup | cache.cacheMemory = 64; |
| Set memory available for images. This should typically be around 1/3 of your total RAM. | startup | diskCache.cacheMemory = 64; |
| Maximum size of the disk cache. | startup | diskCache.cacheSize = 512; |
| Location of the disk cache. | startup | diskCache.cacheLocation = "/var/tmp/Shake/cache"; |
| Set maximum viewer resolution. This setting does not affect files written to disk | startup | gui.viewer.maxWidth = 4096; gui.viewer.maxHeight = 4096; |
| Controls whether or not you are using the full UNC file path. 1 means yes, 0 means no. | startup | script.uncFileNames = 1; |
| Add a favorite directory in the File Browser. The / at the end of the path is required. | ui | nuiFileBrowserAddFavorite ("/icons/scr/"); nuiFileBrowserAddFavorite ("$proj/"); |
| Sets your default browsing point when you launch Shake. | ui | gui.fileBrowser.lastImageDir= "/pix/" ; gui.fileBrowser.lastScriptDir = "$MYPROJ/scripts/" ; |
| Number of node columns in  each function tab (Image, Color, Filter, etc.). | startup | gui.doBoxColumns = 8 |

Interface

Image

Color

Filter

Key

Layer

Transform

Warp

Other

Scripting

Customizing

Keyboard

## Common Macro Modifications

| Action | Folder | Code |
|---|---|---|
| Create an on/off button for a parameter. | ui | NuxDefExprToggle ("Node.parameter"); |
| Set the slider range for a parameter. | ui | NuiDefSlider ("Node.parameter" , 0, 100, 1); |
| Group parameters into a sub-group. | ui | nuiPushControlGroup("Node.group"); nuiGroupControl("Node.param1" ); nuiGroupControl("Node.param2" ); nuiGroupControl("Node.param3" ); nuiPopControlGroup(); |
| Attach a color picker to a grouped parameter triplet. | ui | nuiPushControlWidget( "Color", nuiConnectColorTriplet( kRGBToggle, kCurrentColor, 1 ) ); |
| Attach radio buttons to a parameter. | ui | nuxDefRadioBtnCtrl( "Text.xAlign", 1, 1, 0, "1lux/radio/radio_left", "2lux/radio/radio_center", "3lux/radio/radio_right" ); |

## General Windowing

Stop processing

Toggle Time Code/Frame View
in Time-based displays

Update the Viewer

Expand view from
quarter to full-screen
(and return)

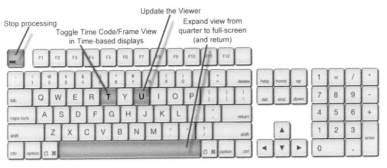

Mouse shortcuts:

Pan image

Zoom windows

Tear off selected
tab as floating
window

## Viewer Workspace

Toggle A/B
Image Buffers

Toggle Color   Toggle Viewer
Channels      Scripts

Toggle Update       Toggle Compare
Mode                Mode

Zoom Image
in Viewer

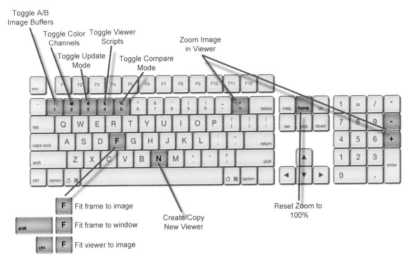

F   Fit frame to image

shift   F   Fit frame to window

ctrl   F   Fit viewer to image

Create/Copy
New Viewer

Reset Zoom to
100%

Mouse shortcuts:

option   LMB Drag   Pan image

## The MultiPlane Viewer

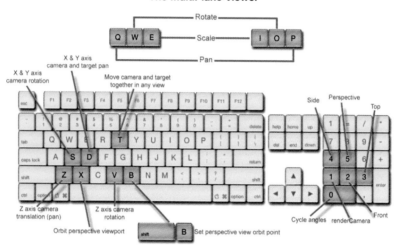

## The Curve Editor

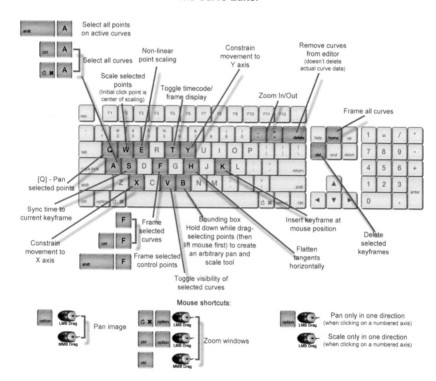

# Flipbooks

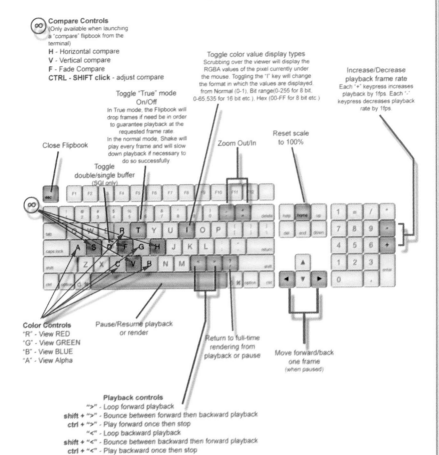

**Compare Controls**
(Only available when launching a "compare" flipbook from the terminal)
**H** - Horizontal compare
**V** - Vertical compare
**F** - Fade Compare
**CTRL - SHIFT click** - adjust compare

**Toggle color value display types**
Scrubbing over the viewer will display the RGBA values of the pixel currently under the mouse. Toggling the 'I' key will change the format in which the values are displayed. from Normal (0-1), Bit range(0-255 for 8 bit, 0-65.535 for 16 bit etc.), Hex (00-FF for 8 bit etc.)

**Increase/Decrease playback frame rate**
Each "+" keypress increases playback by 1fps. Each "-" keypress decreases playback rate by 1fps.

**Toggle "True" mode On/Off**
In True mode, the Flipbook will drop frames if need be in order to guarantee playback at the requested frame rate.
In the normal mode, Shake will play every frame and will slow down playback if necessary to do so successfully

**Zoom Out/In**

**Reset scale to 100%**

**Close Flipbook**

**Toggle double/single buffer**
(SGI only)

**Color Controls**
"R" - View RED
"G" - View GREEN
"B" - View BLUE
"A" - View Alpha

**Pause/Resume playback or render**

**Return to full-time rendering from playback or pause**

**Move forward/back one frame**
(when paused)

**Playback controls**
">" - Loop forward playback
**shift + ">"** - Bounce between forward then backward playback
**ctrl + ">"** - Play forward once then stop
"<" - Loop backward playback
**shift + "<"** - Bounce between backward then forward playback
**ctrl + "<"** - Play backward once then stop

Interface    Image    Color    Filter    Key    Layer    Transform    Warp    Other    Scripting    Customizing    Keyboard

# The Curve Editor

## The Node View

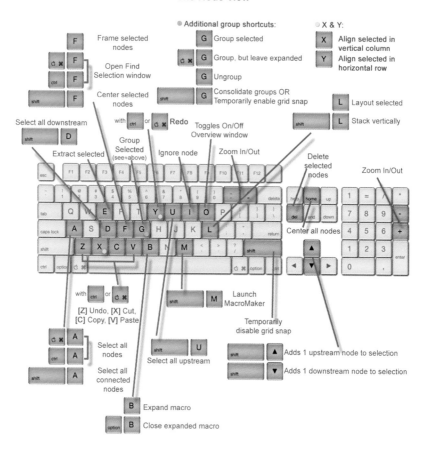

**Frame selected nodes** — F

**Open Find Selection window** — ⇧⌘ F / ctrl F

**Center selected nodes** — shift F

**Additional group shortcuts:** ●
- **Group selected** — G
- **Group, but leave expanded** — ⇧⌘ G
- **Ungroup** — G
- **Consolidate groups OR Temporarily enable grid snap** — shift G

**X & Y:** ○
- **Align selected in vertical column** — X
- **Align selected in horizontal row** — Y

**Layout selected** — L
**Stack vertically** — shift L

**Select all downstream** — shift D

**Redo** — with ctrl or ⇧⌘

**Toggles On/Off Overview window**

**Group Selected** (see ● above)

**Extract selected**

**Ignore node**

**Zoom In/Out**

**Delete selected nodes**

**Zoom In/Out**

**Center all nodes**

**with ctrl or ⇧⌘**
**[Z] Undo, [X] Cut, [C] Copy, [V] Paste**

**Launch MacroMaker** — shift M

**Temporarily disable grid snap**

**Select all nodes** — ⇧⌘ A / ctrl A

**Select all connected nodes** — shift A

**Select all upstream** — shift U

**Adds 1 upstream node to selection** — shift ▲

**Adds 1 downstream node to selection** — shift ▼

**Expand macro** — B

**Close expanded macro** — option B